EAT LIKE
YOU
GIVE A FORK

EAT LIKE YOU GIVE A FORK

THE REAL DISH ON EATING TO THRIVE

MAREYA IBRAHIM

St. Martin's Griffin
New York

Book Design by Rita Sowins / Sowins Design

www.stmartins.com

The Library of Congress Cataloging-in-Publication Data is available upon request.

ISBN 978-1-250-18977-6 (paper over board)
ISBN 978-1-250-30441-4 (ebook)

Our books may be purchased in bulk for promotional, educational, or business use. Please contact your local bookseller or the Macmillan Corporate and Premium Sales Department at 1-800-221-7945, extension 5442, or by email at MacmillanSpecialMarkets@macmillan.com.

First Edition: June 2019

10 9 8 7 6 5 4 3 2 1

TO MES PETITS CHOUX
SOFIA, LUCCA, AND GABE:
YOU FEED MY HEART AND SOUL.
I HOPE TO ALWAYS KEEP YOU FULL!

CONTENTS

ACKNOWLEDGMENTS

Growing up, my scientist father thought television was a complete waste of time. We only had access to three channels on our rabbit-eared box, and the only one he acknowledged wouldn't rot our brains was PBS. On any given day, the options were *NOVA, Animal Kingdom*, or Julia Child. I thought she was so quirky and kind of odd, and had to be seven feet tall because she just towered over all her guests, including Jacques Pépin, who was at least six feet tall, right?

Yet after a while, Julia Child started to grow on me, and soon she became my mentor from afar. I would watch her explain and gesture and eat, and her passion just oozed like cream out of a cannoli. There are foodies, and then there are people who sweat butter and breathe olive oil. Julia for defined passion—for ingredients, the art of cooking, the people around her, and for bringing people to the table. I couldn't get enough of her goofball charm, and her zest for lemons and life was the flavor that made learning from her so incredibly . . . tangy.

The quotes you can find of Julia quipping about cuisine could fill a book on their own, but the one that always gets me in the gut really has nothing to do with food: "Remember, no one's more important than people! In other words, friendship is the most important thing—not career or housework, or one's fatigue—and it needs to be nurtured."

This book is dedicated to the pursuit of nurturing the relationships that feed your soul and giving you the fuel to thrive. It's not about hours and hours slaving away in the kitchen, hurting your brain trying to figure out what and how to eat, or getting down on yourself because you just can't stomach another juice fast.

Instead, this is about adopting a way of life that becomes a celebration. Each and every bite you take can become a party, an occasion worth toasting—sans toast. If you follow the road map of the eight strategies I outline in this book and allow your taste buds to take flight, you may soon discover that everything else in your life starts to feel different. If you shift your relationship with your plate, you can shift your personal relationships, your self-confidence, your intuition, your consciousness, your body, your mood, and your destiny. It's that dramatic. The tens of thousands of people I have spoken to, coached, or mentored could not have even imagined what they could do to get their lives back without making these strategies part of their everyday lives.

I could never have embarked upon this road without so many significant people in my life. To my mother, Janette, and my father, Shawki, who sacrificed everything that was comfortable to bring their children from Egypt to the U.S. for a chance at a better life; to my brother, Daniel, for always being wise beyond his years and the person I can always dish with. To the people who helped make this book possible: Greg Ray, my incredible agent who believed so strongly in my vision to get me there; Teri Lyn Fisher, for photographing the foods in this book so beautifully; Wilmarose Orleans, for her incredible approach to styling the dishes in a "real" way; Sally Cameron, my good friend and talented chef assistant, for her technical chops. And to my children, Sofia and Lucca—you are my light, my breath, my inspiration, and the very reason why this book has come to be my third child. And to my Fit Tribe, who have watched, read, and supported me through all my foodie endeavors, this mouthful is for you. God, you're my #1!

INTRODUCTION: STEP UP TO THE PLATE

You Hot Dish, You!

I get you like no one else. You're fed up. This body of yours doesn't come with an owner's manual, so you've played the diet game like a bad online dating site and nothing has quite "lit your fire." You tried going Paleo but got the worst constipation ever, and there's still bacon fat splattered on the ceiling. You went raw vegan and got tired of eating everything cold and getting the cold shoulder from your family after you canceled pizza night. So you tried the dairy-free, grain-free, bean-free, nut-free, fat-free, taste-free diet intermittently, ate with only chopsticks, and got so hungry you got splinters in your teeth. Worse, your fridge is the sad home to a few empty ketchup packets, diet soda, and moldy takeout from two weeks ago. You've tried the bazillion fad diet plans out there, and none of them has worked, because guess what, cutie pie...No one should do anything that starts with "die."

The very word *diet* probably sends chills down your spine because it suggests deprivation, despair, and a flavorless death sentence. Why should you inflict that on yourself when life is hard enough, and all you want right now are some French fries cooked in duck fat and a killer double chocolate chip macadamia chunk cookie?

For Fork's Sake!

It can be hot, sweet, smoky, spicy, and raw. It's yummy. It's sensual, and it can bring you to tears. It's fun, too—so fun that most people do it three times a day. Food is magical. It's a miracle of nature. It expresses culture. It brings us together for celebration. It feeds our intellect and our creativity. It fuels the ability to cope, manage stress, and make critical decisions. It has an alchemic ability to make us giddy with joy, especially when there's chocolate involved. It forms the building blocks of our DNA, *for fork's sake*, so what you eat today will actually affect your offspring. (If you haven't had kids yet, drop the Doritos!) There's even a component of food that affects our genetic expression that helps determine how long our lives will be and how well we might live them. The truth is, food can completely change your destiny, and the fork in the road is always "Eat right." So why is eating so *forking* confusing?

Something happened to us as a society right around the end of World War II when we entered into the Cold War. Manufacturers began making *phood*—you know, that chemically injected, processed fake food that could survive nuclear devastation unaltered.

Processed beef and pork by-products molded into a square, canned anything, and cellophane-wrapped cakes with an infinite shelf life were bomb-shelter favorites and made their way into the hearts and clogged arteries of Americans everywhere. Sadly, these complex chemistry experiments with ingredient lists a paragraph long quickly bulked up our grocery store shelves. Did we ever stop to ask ourselves, "Should we be eating it if it can never decompose? Won't it do the same once it gets inside my body?"

I'm happy to report that the Cold War is officially over. It's been over for quite some time. . . . But you'd never know by all the products packed with preservatives lining the shelves. So if our diets become full of fresh food that has a finite shelf life—mostly fruits and vegetables, lean protein and high-quality fats, we'd be eating the right things on the food chain. Like what our great-great-great-grandparents ate. Seems pretty logical, right?

It's time to get real.

Are You Ready for the Real Dish?

I'm Mareya Ibrahim, the Fit Foodie—chef, holistic nutritionist, award-winning entrepreneur, and your new BFF in the kitchen. For more than twenty-five years, I've studied, cooked, tested, grown, trialed, guinea-pigged, and picked apart every calorie of food I could get my hands on. Do you know what I discovered? We've become so obsessed with what *not* to eat and what *not* to do that we've drained the living *fork* out of food!

If you couldn't tell by now, we're about to start a real conversation about what eats us alive when it comes to our feeding habits. There's no shame in this game.

Can I get an *F* yeah?! For all the *F* words associated with food, including *fear*, *fat*, *factories*, *failure*, and *forbidden*, there are a million others that we should focus on, like *friends*, *family*, *fabulous*, *fulfilling*, *fat* (you'll soon read why), *flavor*, and *FUN*. Food has the power to take our emotions to places we've never experienced. It helps us recall memories and reminds us of people. It's a language that doesn't require translation. It's the only art form that lets us taste, see, touch, smell, and hear, inviting us to engage all five senses in the celebration of sustenance.

The good and bad news is, we have the freedom of choice. We hold in our hands the gift of opposable thumbs, and we're able to select what we want to eat from a plethora of abundance versus what's available to pick, gather, or hunt. It gives us a sense of entitlement that, until relatively recently, we'd never experienced in the history of man. Introduce spice, a flame, or another ingredient, and all of a sudden we graduate from simply eating to an expression of magic. That makes us alchemists, kitchen magicians. The real trick is, we can breathe a different kind of life into our humanity when our sustenance is created with intention and quality.

If "you are what you eat," I don't think any one of us wants to be thought of as fast or cheap, or described as "okay, but I've had better."

Growing up, the ultimate expression of love from the many matriarchs of my family was imposing food on everyone until we couldn't move. Food was the way they showed their adoration. Because they were so loving and generous, they wouldn't let you leave the table until you had eaten half your body weight. Your gut would feel like it was about to burst, and who feels motivated to slay the day after that? A nap was about the only thing you could physically handle. As for self-confidence, well, there's nothing sexy about feeling like a ten-ton sack of potatoes. I developed a really unhealthy relationship with food that left me swinging the opposite direction, never wanting to eat for fear of how horrible I would feel afterward.

At one point, I actually said I'd rather take a pill than eat again so I wouldn't have to think about it. *Gasp.* I shudder to think of such blasphemy.

The truth is, the bad feelings were eating me alive, and through my health coaching, I quickly found out that a lot of other people could relate. That's why I dedicated myself to figuring out how to help people avoid getting stuck in the muck of guilt and frustration. Here's what I concluded and confirmed through success after success story—(it's going to rotate your plate): You don't have to label yourself or wear your food habits as a badge of martyrdom. You don't have to avoid whole food groups. You get to stop counting points. Maybe most important, you can let go of, for the rest of your life, the mental gymnastics you experience deciding what to eat.

Our relationship with food shouldn't be torturous. It shouldn't be a "put up with it" deal or one of sacrificial desperation, using the gym to pay penance for all the crap we've eaten. Two hundred push-ups, five miles on the treadmill, and a few Hail Marys for eating half a pan of brownies. Food is so much more than the bites. It is cumulative information that feeds that cpu (central processing unit) of yours. Dr. Mark Hyman says, "Food is the code that programs your biology. You can literally upgrade or downgrade your biological software with every single bite."

In other words, every bite becomes a byte of *you*.

Your internal processor does not compute chemical junkstorms of artificially flavored, highly processed, empty-calorie food and drinks. That's the real reason you can never, ever out-train a bad diet: because what you ingest gets metabolized and either contributes to your health or hurts it. If it was only about calories in, calories out, you could just eat four or five candy bars every day and feel and look amazing. Instead, you'd potentially be starving your body and putting it into a prediabetic state—not to mention wrecking your skin, destroying your gut health, and encouraging heart disease along the way. And just because it's gluten-free, vegan, Paleo, organic, or any other label doesn't mean it's offering you any real benefit. A label is just that. It's a guideline, and I've met many processed-soy vegans and bacon-drenched Paleo people who would not be categorized as healthy by any stretch of the imagination.

It's a clean eating slate that gets wiped today.

When you Eat Like You Give a Fork, the amazing machine called your body reboots and takes over. But first, you have to train it—just like you would if you were getting ready for a marathon after only ever running a 5K or having never put on running shoes in your life. If you just started running full bore, you'd probably tap out after the first hundred yards. . . . I want you in it for the long haul.

We are all different with varied requirements to fuel our fabulous physiques. I'm all of five feet nothin', so if I told you what I eat and expect you—a five-foot-seven, twenty-eight-year-old mom trying to get her body back after pregnancy, or a six-foot-four, forty-nine-year-old male triathlete training for peak performance, or my twelve-year-old son who has two hollow legs—to follow the same caloric plan, you might feel a little "hangry." I can tell you this, though: The core concepts are the same, and that's going to be our focus.

The three biggest bonuses?

1. **Carbs and fat are not only included, they're required.**
2. **You eat four or five times a day.**
3. **Enjoy a "last meal," the kind you think of as a cheat, three times a week.**

This is your invitation to take a seat at a new kind of chef's table. One that invites honest, healthy dishing, a set of strategies that allow you flexibility in this real world of ours, and recipes that won't keep you in the kitchen all day.

Now hang on, 'cause I'm prepared to break down the bull for you like a master butcher.

Shift Gets Real

Over the last ten years, I've dialed in the "secret sauce" that has brought people jaw-dropping results—turning back the clock five, ten, twenty years. You see it, you feel it, and all of a sudden, the *shift* gets real. In this book, I'll immerse you in my Eight Essential Strategies that will remake your kitchen, your taste buds, your body, your energy level, and your relationships—all making you a *forkin'* happy person. It never ceases to amaze me, but when you get your food house in order, your joy factor and proclivity to thrive naturally goes through the roof.

The core elements that make up this book were developed over my *looooong* food career helping others create the exact environment where they could succeed in losing weight, reducing inflammation, and becoming the rock stars that God created them to be. This is not about food shaming, fat shaming, shape shaming, or any other perceptions around controlling our food choices. It is simply about honoring your body, your mind, and your psyche with a real-food plan that gets you to your realistic goals.

#LifeGoals

To stick with anything, having the right motivation is *everything*.

So, what's your *why*? I learned long ago that you need to always have a BAG—a "big amazing goal" that keeps you motivated like a hungry dog chasing a big amazing bone. What is lighting your fire to make the shift happen?

- **Do you want enough energy to keep up with your kids? Grandkids?**
- **Do you dream about fitting into a favorite piece of clothing again?**
- **Did you have a health scare that got you in touch with your mortality?**
- **Are you tired of feeling sick and tired, and dragging through the day like you're pulling a bag of rocks?**

This is all about you, so keep it very personal and specific. Put your BAG goal somewhere you can see it. Write it on your mirror. Make a note on your smartphone. Make it your screensaver. Post it on Pinterest, Instagram, and Facebook. Make it your mantra, and let that be the fuel to torch your doubt, fear, and negative self-talk. No more excuses: Not your age. Not your gender. Not your relationship status. Not your bank account. No more excuses!

I-8-2
INFINITY

We make about 35,000 decisions every day, 1,050,000 in the average month, and 12,775,000 in a year. Multiply that by 38,000 items in an average grocery store, and you're probably so decision-fatigued, your eyes are like glazed donut holes. No wonder we all look like a bunch of zombies from *The Walking Dead* meandering the cereal aisle! With every bite, you're making a critically important choice, because those bites impact your future. You are constantly in a state of *becoming* through your blood chemistry (feeding a stable blood sugar level that doesn't send you into a cycle of spike and plunge), tissue renewal (certain foods actually feed your cell walls and replication), and energy (are you burning quality food that is a source of clean energy, or are you burning trash, which lights up quickly but has no staying power?).

You are not on a diet when you Eat Like You Give a Fork. You're living a sustainable lifestyle that feeds your sanity, fuels your vitality, and sets your metabolism on fire. There is nothing more stressful, mentally and physically, than trying to reinvent what your body requires you to do daily not only to survive but also to thrive. Did you know that most fights happen with loved ones one hour before dinnertime? No "hangry" person with low blood sugar or restrictive dieter is in a position to play nice or make rational decisions.

That series of choices starts with my Eight Essential Food Strategies, which you practice, eat, and repeat. Put the number 8 on its side, and it becomes the infinity symbol. You'll learn how to quit wasting food, time, and money for a lifetime, and how to heal your body and spirit, creating the most vibrant version of *you*. Is that not *fan-forkin'-tastic*?!

My hope is that this book becomes your go-to guide, your owner's manual—your bae. We all need a clear road map to keep the id—the pleasure-hound part of the psyche that just wants to eat every fried piece of sugar within reach—from going completely AWOL. You wouldn't get on a plane and travel without having an itinerary or an idea of where you're headed, but most people try to navigate unknown food territory without speaking the language or accessing Google Translate. Here's some real food for thought. The terms *gluten-free*, *organic*, *all-natural*, *low-fat*, *sugar-free*, and *zero-calorie* don't mean squat if

there's no substance behind the package. And the right solutions won't just jump into your cart or out of your fridge screaming, "Put a fork in me!" I'm going to show you how to own your destiny with realistic, sustainable eating habits and recipes with a solid foundation.

Your Body, Your House

At the center of this concept of eating like you give a fork is learning how to retrain your taste buds, the most powerful, potentially unruly, muscle in your hot bod. The tongue wags the dog. No matter how many good-for-you foods you put in front of yourself or others, you have to learn to like the flavors that keep you healthy first, or else it's always going to be take-out pizza time. Most people's taste buds have formed by the time they're three years old. If all you were conditioned to eat were Hot Pockets and corn dogs, without a fresh veg in sight, guess what, buttercup: The concept of kale or the thought of putting spinach in your blender might make you convulse. Or cry. I've had people tell me their significant others gave them ultimatums: "It's either me or the tofu." It doesn't have to be your husband or the processed soy, loves. It just has to be real food. Really *forkin'* good food.

The nutritionally balanced recipes, quick tips, and techniques presented in *Eat Like You Give a Fork* take the I'll-just-feed-my-face feeling out of food and replace it with intentional, exciting, flavorful, yummy dishes. I wear a shirt that says "Think before you bite." It means, eat food consciously.

> You'll start to see your cravings—the ones that have you by the Sno Balls—change pronto, and with that, you will start to prefer what is naturally better for you.

No mindless munching, maniacal multitasking, or what I call "fridge *forking*"—you know, standing in front of the refrigerator and using your fork to taste-test everything in sight. We're also putting an end to succumbing to the empty promises of an empty calorie food label just because you were hungry. One of the biggest shifts you'll experience is that your cravings—the ones that have you buy the Sno Balls—change pronto, and with that, you will start to prefer what is naturally better for you. The idea of slicing into a pile of biscuits and gravy or inhaling a deep-fried whipped cream–injected yellow cake will have you shuddering, and you'll be able to avoid a 911 food emergency situation that has you stress-scarfing. You'll plan, shop, and eat with intention.

While all eight strategies are essential to this plan, the simple, real recipes are what will help you stay on track. You can look endlessly through books and online, amassing Pinterest-worthy how-tos or untested recipes that sound good on your screen but don't work and don't necessarily help you understand how to eat in a nutritionally and macronutrient-balanced way. The ease of preparation, the baked-in nutrition, and the "cheffy" touches change how people eat for a lifetime—not just as some temporary quick fix that doesn't fix anything.

The Eight Essential Strategies are for the whole you. The you who is caught living a hectic, on-the-go existence that may be eating you alive. You are the whole package, and through whole foods and a whole approach, you can find greater joy, feel ridiculously amazing, and rock this life you've been given by squeezing the juice out of every day.

THE EIGHT ESSENTIAL STRATEGIES

STRATEGY 1:
Retrain Your Taste Buds

STRATEGY 2:
The Real Kitchen

STRATEGY 3:
Get Up on Greens

STRATEGY 4:
The Fast Break

STRATEGY 5:
Go Gluten-Free
Super Grains

STRATEGY 6:
Fat Fillers

STRATEGY 7:
Be Real Dense

STRATEGY 8:
The 90/10 Rule

Eating to Thrive

Instead of just feeding the hungry you, we're going to feed the vital you. The *Eat Like You Give a Fork* approach changes the way you make food choices. As its foundation, non-starchy veggies make up 50 percent of your daily volume intake, paired with clean proteins, single-ingredient carbs, fat fillers, and nutrient-dense foods to help you pack in vitamins, minerals, and critical nutrients, like essential amino acids (EAAs). These EAAs are boldly referred to as the building blocks of life because they're *that* important. Bodybuilders have known about EAAs for years and manipulated them for optimal performance. The truth is, they're critical to your ability to thrive. As humans, nine amino acids are considered essential, but as adults, our bodies require eight of them to function properly—and I mean they're mandatory—and our only sources of these essential eight are from food eaten daily, as we don't store EAAs. It would make sense that if these amino acids are at the core of building life, our meals should be based around them, right? According to the UC Davis Integrative Medicine blog, amino acids account for 75 percent of dry body weight, 95 percent of muscle (including your heart), and 100 percent of hormones, neurotransmitters, and neuropeptides (the pilots and air traffic controllers of your nervous system that keep you from crashing or ending up in Cuba when you were headed for Miami).

For instance, without the EAA phenylalanine, you wouldn't be able to regulate your thyroid or metabolism. Without lysine, you would have a really hard time keeping your immunity and antibodies in check. Without tryptophan, you couldn't produce serotonin, the feel-good hormone that makes you feel turned on and helps you sleep. And unlike fat and starch, our bodies can't store EAAs for a rainy day, so getting them daily is critical to your well-being. I repeat: In order to keep all this fabulosity together, your meals need to be offering you the full range of nutrients, including EAAs. This is where *Eat Like You Give a Fork* will become your owner's manual for fit foodiness, where nutrition and cheffy-ness meet at the corner of nom-nom.

Foods, especially those containing complete EAAs, can give you superpowers when you need strength, build muscle and bones as you age, and support mental acuity for all you do. We can unlock the fountain of youth with food. If you embrace and follow these eight strategies, your weight will reset, your mood will improve, your outlook will get rosier, your skin will glow, you'll eliminate better, you'll have energy to be active—and I guarantee there will be way better boom-chicka-wa-wa.

With the Eight Essential Strategies, you automatically get the eight EAAs woven into most of the recipes to feed the whole you. Maybe the best news is, you'll never get bored mixing up the options. Even if you have legitimate dietary restrictions, you won't miss a "beet" with my carefully orchestrated recipes and suggestions for modification. Just shuffle, eat, and repeat

My goal is that you reach your BAG by saying, "I-8-2 infinity." Now let's get crackin'.

THE EIGHT ESSENTIAL AMINO ACIDS

All animal-based foods contain the essential eight amino acids—so pretty much every animal protein, eggs, seafood, and dairy will encompass these—but plant protein and certain foods are richer than others, or can be combined to include a full range of essential AAs. If you can't remember what plant-based foods provide the complete spectrum, remember, quinoa is the bomb and beans and rice are oh so nice!

TRYPTOPHAN	Seaweed, Soy Protein, Sesame Seeds, Crab Meat, Spinach, Corn, Legumes, Grains, Mozzarella Cheese
ISOLEUCINE	Fish, Eggs, Turkey, Chicken, Soy Protein, Nuts, Most Seeds, Bean Sprouts
METHIONINE	Eggs, Seafood, Chicken, Buffalo, Turkey, Peas, Mushrooms
THREONINE	Greek Yogurt, Eggs, Nuts, Beans, Seeds, Broccoli, Avocado
VALINE	Edamame, Nuts/Nut Butters, Spinach, Quinoa, Seeds, Artichokes
PHENYLALANINE	Oats, Tofu, Hemp Seeds, Chia Seeds, Nuts, Soy Protein Isolate, Asparagus
LEUCINE	Buckwheat, Tempeh, Natto, Nuts, Pumpkin Seeds, Tuna, White Beans
LYSINE	Fish, Legumes, Nuts, Avocado, Kale, Brussels Sprouts, Quinoa

RETRAIN YOUR TASTE BUDS

Let's get real. No judgment, ok?

You choose peanut butter and jelly on white bread, gummy worms, and Cocoa Puffs. Dinner looks like hot dogs, burgers, pizza, and mac 'n' cheese. Throw in some pancakes and bacon, Goldfish, and Oreos washed down with Kool-Aid, and you've got your ideal meal. Not *one* identifiable vegetable in there. So basically, your taste buds never advanced beyond preschool. Or maybe you got to grade school–level taste buds, where you can stomach a few celery sticks with ranch dressing alongside your Buffalo wings, but the idea of a salad or grilled fish makes you break out in a clammy sweat. Maybe this isn't you but someone you live with?

Look, it's not your fault. Blame it on your parents. It all starts in the womb. If Mama was washing down Twinkies and chips with diet soda from fifteen weeks on, that impacted your taste buds when you were just swimming around in there, because you were swallowing about a liter of amniotic fluid every trimester. Then you made your exit and got introduced to the perfect food—mother's milk. Then you sprouted teeth and your free will set in, and, well, once a child has a nuclear meltdown over broccoli, it's easy for a parent to let go of the wheel. The good news is, it's never too late to help your taste buds grow up.

Why We Slip Down the Rainbow

My son was a phenomenal eater as a baby. He'd slurp up his sweet potatoes and pound his peas. Apples were his favorite, and he'd down the pureed pears and plums like a champ. But when he turned two, the little tyrant started throwing down the gauntlet at every meal.

Children have the ability to express their displeasure with foods from a very early age, whether by spitting it out, throwing it on the floor or across the room, or painting the walls and the ceiling with it. That was my son. Anything green flew from his mouth in a projectile explosion that left us both ugly sobbing. It was gruesome, and many peas paid the price.

After our little ones make the transition from the wondrous, complete nutrition that is breast milk to solid food, they soon shift to fruit and veggies—peas, carrots, spinach, green beans, squash, you name it. Yet somewhere between veggie-full plates and the age of ordering off a children's menu, the palette of red, orange, green, purple, and blue morphs to brown, then slips to white. The color drains from the plate like the face of a person about to faint and we are quicker to accept brown and white food as the mainstay in order to avoid a full-out battle.

Why do we slip down the rainbow to the point of no palate return? It's called *neophobia*, a fear aroused by new foods, and it's a common syndrome. All omnivorous animals are scared to try the unknown. The years between the ages of two and ten are the worst, and between four and seven years, children usually only agree to taste something unfamiliar if they are strongly encouraged to, not threatened. Neophobia can be overcome with education and consistency. That means sticking with it and offering new foods up to twenty times without giving in to the tantrums and fits.

The average person is born with about ten thousand taste buds, which explains why certain foods may taste stronger to children and why accepting different flavor profiles can be so challenging. But don't despair! About every two weeks during childhood, taste buds get replaced, so foods your kid spit across the room one week might be their jam a month later. If you let off the gas and don't keep filling their plate with veggies—whether they throw them across the room or not —it'll be much harder to introduce varied flavors later on. Dr. Daniel Amen, author of the *New York Times* bestseller *The Daniel Plan* (to which I had the honor of contributing), says, "You have to be their frontal lobe until theirs develops."

A growing process is happening—give it time to put down roots before you pull it up. And if you need to, feel free to have another glass of wine as your kids or significant other throws a tantrum over the tomatoes—and keep breathing.

Drop and Give Me Twenty Tongue Dips

Taste buds are highly complex structures. Thousands of them respond to temperature, and the physical sensations from food or drink coupled with smell send signals to the brain and ignite a perception—savory, sweet, acidic, acrid, bland, salty, balanced, and the range in between. Just like muscles, those taste buds need to be conditioned, tested, and strengthened so they can take on a broad spectrum of those flavors. This doesn't mean you have to quit the less-healthy foods you love cold turkey. It simply means you're diversifying and developing a taste for more nutrient-dense sustenance.

Flexing your taste buds means retraining them with the same focus and energy that you would use if you were strength training at the gym. By developing a taste for the sour, bitter, and umami—the taste profile that is often described as meaty or savory and is the result of a combination of amino acids—you'll learn to love foods such as spinach and other nutritious greens, celery, seaweed, citrus, fish, mushrooms, and tomatoes, which will forever change how you eat and will help you naturally fight disease. We'll transform how you build your meals, reset your taste buds, and refine your waistline, starting the minute you open your eyes in the morning. Dedicating half your plate to nonstarchy veggies will help you crush your Forkin' Good goals.

You'll often hear someone describe themselves as having a sweet tooth. They finish a meal and start craning their necks, looking for the dessert tray, or spooning with the Chunky Monkey. Is it a habit or a true physiological need for sugar? It could be a little bit of both, if you aren't getting enough protein or fat in your meals. What you eat for breakfast sets the tone for the day. Just think, if you start your day with a pile of pancakes doused in syrup, donuts, or even the perceived healthy option of sweetened yogurt with honey-laden granola, you train your taste buds to crave sugar and starchy foods for the rest of your waking moments. It's kind of a U.S. thing, because when you look around the world, you find that most countries start their day savory.

In Japan, breakfast is sea vegetables, rice, and raw fish. In China, it's congee, a rice porridge that can be seasoned with mushrooms or pork, among other things. In Egypt, it's stewed brown fava beans with hummus, tahini, eggs, and pickled turnips. In Sweden, they'll have slabs of whole-grain cracker bread with slices of cheese, pâté, and pickles. In Spain, it's bread rubbed with garlic and tomato. In India, it might be lentil dosas with sour chutney or a spicy lentil dal soup. In Australia, you can get your Vegemite on toast. In Mongolia, the day wouldn't start on the right foot without boiled mutton. In Uganda, they eat stewed bananas and cow organs. In the Bahamas, a plate of spicy prawns and grits is the breakfast of champions. And in Peru, ceviche made with raw, marinated seafood is a typical starter for the day.

At a typical hotel breakfast buffet, you can get a stack of pancakes, cornflakes, chocolate milk, Danishes, muffins, waffles, toast, pound cake, and a variety of juices to wash it down with—and then go into a sugar coma.

> It's never too late to help your taste buds grow up.

The same person who grew up eating sea vegetables and raw fish in Japan can acclimate to the sugary American diet in a heartbeat, but to go the opposite way takes a little more persuasion and time. Just look at where those taste buds sit on the tongue! The ones that crave sugar and salt are hanging out just at the tip, waiting to get their jollies on cookies, cake, and candy with a salt lick chaser. When you look at the physiological aspect of taste cravings, you begin to understand why it takes intentionality and brainpower to make the best choices. You can retrain your taste buds and lick the crazy cravings with our reset.

Flex That Tongue Like a Champ

That tongue has a mind of its own, and if it had its way, it would be dipping its little papillae into sugar and salt all day. So it's time to wake up what's been in hibernation for a *looooong* time. In our reset, we are gradually going to retrain your taste buds by conditioning them to crave umami, bitter, and sour flavors so your desire and cravings for cleaner eating eventually take flight. Fermented and vinegar-based preparations, spices, and amino acids will play a big role.

When you retrain your taste buds, you also retrain your brain to crave different foods, and before you know it, you'll see your plate from a different perspective. Imagine picking broccoli and Brussels sprouts over brownies. Through this eating plan, you'll begin to actually crave—and even lust after—greens, fermented foods, and umami everything in your daily routine. Yes, I said "lust"!

The enlightenment of knowing what your body needs and feeding it properly is a next-level game-changer. It will shift your mood, your energy level, how you handle stress, how you deal with your relationships, your ability to sleep, and every other aspect of your consciousness. You will crave good things. You'll become stronger than you've ever felt, and you'll develop a deeper appreciation for that incredible temple of yours. It's *that* powerful, and I want you to experience it firsthand.

Now, you wouldn't expect a person trying to get fit at the gym to bench press 200 pounds off the bat or start showing off a six-pack in a week. Metamorphosis happens easily with our eight-day plan, because you have to rewire your tongue-to-brain connection to enable eating success. Just keep in mind that it can take trying a food up to twenty times before you develop a taste for it, so give peas a chance. Most of all, you will be giving your body a steady supply of nutrient-dense deliciousness while weaning yourself off the damaging effects of eating sugar, salt, and too much unhealthy fat. Just think of me as your taste bud coach, building a stronger muscle in the kitchen instead of the gym. You'll be flexing that tongue like a world-class bodybuilder in no time. . . . And if abs are made in the kitchen, it makes sense to start here, right?

Are you ready to unlock the gateway to a whole new world of health and wellness? Every day for eight days, you'll be exploring at least five flavor combinations for a reason. In these flights, you'll experience how to hone your taste bud champions and quell the assassins, the ones that kill your quest for health. I provide the recipe/preparation for the reconditioning tasting flight along with my full list of food tips for loosening the grip that flab-forming flavors can have on your brain and body.

THE ALL-YOU-CAN-EAT BUFFET

What if I told you there are some foods you could eat all you wanted, as much as you wanted, every day, without even so much as counting a calorie? This is the FREEBIE list, the All-You-Can-Eat buffet, the pile it high and wide list, so get to chompin'. You will never be hangry again.

- Artichokes
- Asparagus
- Bean sprouts
- Bell peppers
- Broccoli
- Brussels sprouts
- Cabbage
- Cauliflower
- Celery
- Cucumber
- Eggplant
- Fennel
- Green peas

- Greens (lettuce, spinach, chard, arugula, kale, bok choy, etc.)
- Jicama
- Kohlrabi
- Leeks
- Mushrooms
- Radishes
- Snap peas
- Tomatoes
- Turnips
- Yellow squash
- Zucchini

- Build your plate starting with nonstarchy veggies. Any of the veggies from "The All-You-Can-Eat Buffet" (page 18) are suggested.
- In the morning, start with protein and fat and avoid sugary foods to stabilize your blood sugar. This can include any of my egg dishes, chia seed pudding (yes, you can have pudding for breakfast), or smoothies made with mostly green veggies and a handful of low-glycemic fruit like berries and apples.
- Combine protein, fat, and complex carbs in every meal, focusing on bitter, sour, and umami flavors.
- Eat smaller reconditioning meals every three to four hours to keep your energy high, rev your metabolism, and sustain your blood sugar so you never feel hungry. See the Taste Bud Reconditioning Flights (below) for more.
- Enjoy at least one raw or mostly raw meal a day to get the maximum benefit out of your nutrients, enzymes, and probiotics without cooking them off.
- Drink a Real Vitality Tonic (page 47) once a day after Meal 1 for eight days.
- Drink some Low-Sodium Umami Bone Broth (page 44) in the mid-afternoon.
- Give your full focus to your food. Sit down, put aside the technology, and eat slowly, tasting every bite. This is your time to fall in love with flavor again.

The Taste Bud Reconditioning Flights

By reconditioning your taste buds, you will be cutting out certain foods and **eating at least five bites each of specific foods** to build that all-powerful muscle. If you'd like, you can dive into the eight-day meal plan that wraps many of these delish flavors together into a well-orchestrated package.

WHAT TO CUT

- All caloric sugar items (including maple syrup, agave, coconut sugar, etc.)
- All breads and bread products (bread, tortillas, pasta, etc.)
- Dairy products (made with cow's milk)
- Processed foods (snack foods, crackers, chips, bars, etc.)
- Artificial sweeteners and colors
- Alcohol
- Soda and juice

WHAT TO FOCUS ON

Eight-Day Tasting Flights: Please eat at least five bites/sips of each of these ingredients daily for eight days. You can enjoy vegetables cooked or raw (for example, enjoy a salad with arugula, tomatoes, mushrooms, spinach, and celery with toasted seaweed strips and the Real Dish Dressing, page 26).

- Tomatoes
- Mushrooms (any variety other than white button)
- Dark leafy greens (spinach, arugula, chard, kale, broccoli, collard greens, etc.)
- Celery
- Avocado
- Toasted seaweed
- Nonvegetarians (pick at least two): natural lean pork, chicken, beef, turkey, bison, wild game, eggs
- Seafood eaters (pick at least two): wild-caught fish, shrimp, mackerel, tuna, anchovies, sardines
- Non–meat eaters (pick at least one): quinoa, seaweed, pickled foods, tempeh, miso, edamame

Eight-Day Taste Bud Reconditioning Meal Plan

If you want to get more advanced with your taste bud reconditioning, eat your way through the dishes and beverages here to boost your taste buds in ways that feed your body to the core.

For eight days, enjoy at least two dishes and one snack each day with Real Vitality Tonic, Low Sodium Bone Broth, and/or You Glow Smoothie. Flex your taste buds and watch that tongue go from flab to fab. These dishes are simple to make and perfect for meal prep; make them once and enjoy for days.

EIGHT-DAY TASTE BUD RESET

DISHES

Th Fork Row Salad

Grilled Artichoke, Hummus, and Napa Cabbage Wraps

Braised Celery Puttanesca

Kaniwa Tabouli with Parsley, Tomato, and Kale

Zucchini Noodles with Romesco Sauce

MedMex Taco Lettuce Cups

Poached Egg and Veggie Brekkie Bowl

Heirloom Tomato, Cucumber, Feta, and Dill Salad with Pumpkin Seed Oil Vinaigrette

SNACKS

Roasted Spiced Almonds

Sun-Dried Tomato, Basil, and White Bean Dip with Snacking Veggies

Garlic and Rosemary Baked Olives

DRINKS

Real Vitality Tonic

Low-Sodium Umami Bone Broth

You Glow Smoothie

At least half your body weight in ounces of water daily (ex: if you weigh 120 pounds, drink 60 ounces of water). Add cucumber, lemon, and/or lime slices and mint, basil, and/or any other fresh herbs.

After the Reset you'll be rockin' a whole new set of stronger, savvier buds that just can't wait to skinny-dip into more nutrient-dense foods. Bitter, sour, and umami flavors will become your besties, and your cravings won't hijack you in the most inconvenient hours anymore (like when you should be sleeping). You'll also enjoy a more satiated existence, tasting food and reacting to hunger differently—maybe for the first time, ever.

YOU GLOW SMOOTHIE

INGREDIENTS

1 cup plain Greek yogurt (or coconut yogurt, for a vegan swap)

¼ cup unsweetened tart cherry or unsweetened pomegranate juice

½ cup fresh or frozen blueberries

½ cup baby spinach

1 tablespoon ground flaxseed

½ cup crushed ice

DIRECTIONS

Combine all the ingredients and 2 cups water in a high-speed blender and blend on high until smooth. Serve ice-cold, preferably with a straw to suck it down.

THE REAL DISH ROW SALAD

INGREDIENTS

4 cups arugula or baby spinach

1 recipe The Real Dish Dressing (page 26)

16 ounces or 3 (5-ounce) cans canned wild-caught tuna packed in water, drained

Juice of ½ lemon

2 teaspoons minced fresh dill leaves only

Sea salt and freshly ground black pepper

3 cups assorted veggies (shredded carrots, baby heirloom or grape tomatoes, haricots verts, red and yellow bell peppers)

1 cup cooked or canned chickpeas or cannellini beans (drained and rinsed, if canned)

1 avocado, pitted and sliced into small chunks

1 cup grapes, sliced in half

DIRECTIONS

1) In a medium bowl, toss the arugula with 2 tablespoons of the dressing to coat. Arrange the arugula on a large platter as a bed for the other ingredients.

2) In the same bowl you used for the arugula, stir together the tuna, lemon juice, and dill, and season with salt and black pepper.

3) Arrange the tuna salad down the middle of the platter over the arugula. Arrange the veggies, chickpeas, avocado, and grapes in individual rows alongside the tuna.

4) Drizzle the remaining 2 tablespoons dressing over the salad and enjoy!

The Real Dish Dressing

INGREDIENTS

3 tablespoons extra-virgin olive oil or avocado oil

1 tablespoon toasted sesame oil

2 teaspoons amino acids

2 teaspoons fresh lime juice

1 teaspoon grated fresh ginger

1 garlic clove, crushed

DIRECTIONS

In a small bowl or jar with a lid, combine all the ingredients and whisk or shake to incorporate. Store in an airtight container (or the jar) in the refrigerator until ready to use, up to 10 days.

GRILLED ARTICHOKE HUMMUS NAPA CABBAGE WRAPS

INGREDIENTS

8 large napa cabbage leaves

1 cup Grilled Artichoke Hummus (page 29)

2 cups shredded carrots

1 cup julienned Persian cucumbers

1 cup julienned red bell pepper

The Real Dish Dressing (page 26), for serving

DIRECTIONS

1) Bring a medium saucepan of water to a boil. Fill a large bowl with ice and water and set it nearby. Drop the cabbage leaves into the boiling water, then immediately transfer them to the ice water. Let cool, then drain and blot dry.

2) Spread 2 tablespoons of the hummus over the lower third of each cabbage leaf, leaving room to roll from the bottom.

3) Layer the shredded vegetables on top of the hummus, dividing them evenly among the cabbage leaves.

4) Starting from the bottom, roll up the cabbage leaves tightly and secure with a toothpick, if needed.

5) Serve with the dressing for dipping.

Grilled Artichoke Hummus

**MAKES 4 TO 6 SERVINGS
OR 1½ CUPS**

INGREDIENTS

1 (15-ounce) can chickpeas, drained and rinsed

1 (12-ounce) jar grilled artichoke hearts in olive oil, drained, 2 tablespoons oil reserved

½ cup tahini (sesame paste)

2 garlic cloves

2 tablespoons fresh lemon juice

1 teaspoon Himalayan pink salt

½ teaspoon ground cumin

½ teaspoon ground coriander

2 teaspoons chopped fresh parsley

DIRECTIONS

1) Set aside 1 tablespoon of the chickpeas for garnish and put the remaining chickpeas in a food processor. Add the artichokes and 1 tablespoon of the reserved oil from the jar, the tahini, garlic, lemon juice, salt, cumin, coriander, and ¼ cup water and pulse until smooth and creamy. Taste and adjust the seasonings.

2) Transfer the hummus to a serving bowl and drizzle with the remaining 1 tablespoon oil. Garnish with the reserved chickpeas and the parsley. Serve alongside snacking veggies, as a dressing for salads, or as a spread for wraps.

MOROCCAN SPICED CHICKEN LEGS

Ras el hanout is a North African spice mix, the name of which means "head of the shop" or "top shelf" in Arabic (the best spices the shop has to offer). What I love about it is that you pretty much don't need anything else for seasoning. It's got cumin, cardamom, clove, allspice, chile, ginger, turmeric, paprika, and a rainbow of other ingredients, so when you have it on hand, you can use it as a seasoning for shrimp, fish, veggies, tempeh, and anything else your exotic heart desires. Spice blends rock!

INGREDIENTS

2 tablespoons ras el hanout

2 teaspoons garlic powder

1 teaspoon sea salt

1 teaspoon ground white pepper

2 tablespoons raw coconut oil, melted

8 large chicken legs, removing skin is optional

DIRECTIONS

1) Preheat the oven to 400°F. Line a baking sheet with aluminum foil.

2) In a medium bowl, combine the ras el hanout, garlic powder, salt, white pepper, and coconut oil and stir to form a paste. Pat the chicken legs dry and slather them with the spice paste until evenly coated.

3) Place the chicken legs in a single layer on the prepared baking sheet (or in a baking dish), leaving room between them. Cover with foil and bake for about 30 minutes. Remove the foil and bake for 15 to 20 minutes more, until the internal temperature at the thickest point (without touching the bone) reaches 165°F and the skin or flesh is golden brown. Enjoy with Molokhia Soup (page 108) or on their own, hot or at room temperature.

BRAISED CELERY PUTTANESCA

Even though puttanesca reputedly has a sordid past as the dish Italian ladies of the night made for their suitors, this version could be served to anyone with great results. While you'd normally see puttanesca sauce paired with pasta, this one gets tossed with braised celery chunks, which act as a beautiful, meaty base to this dish. Don't worry if you don't like anchovies—they won't overpower the dish, but instead lend it an umami "meatiness" and a slightly salty flavor, along with a nice dose of omega-3s.

INGREDIENTS

¼ cup raw coconut oil

6 anchovy fillets

1 teaspoon red pepper flakes, plus more if desired

3 garlic cloves, crushed

1 tablespoon tomato paste

2 (16-ounce) cans chopped tomatoes

1 tablespoon minced fresh parsley

1 tablespoon capers, drained and rinsed

½ teaspoon freshly ground black pepper

2 pounds celery stalks, tops and bottoms trimmed, cut into 1-inch pieces

DIRECTIONS

1) In a large sauté pan, melt the coconut oil over medium heat. Add the anchovies and red pepper flakes and cook, stirring occasionally, until the anchovies dissolve into the oil, about 2 minutes.

2) Add the garlic and sauté for another minute.

3) Add the tomato paste and cook, stirring, for 1 minute. Add the tomatoes and cook for another minute. Add the parsley, capers, and black pepper and stir to combine.

4) Stir in the celery to coat with the sauce. Reduce the heat to medium-low and cook for 20 minutes, or until the celery is very tender.

5) If you like it spicier, kick up the spice with more red pepper flakes.

MEDMEX LETTUCE CUP TACOS

I call my signature style "MedMex"—it's a fusion of Mediterranean and Mexican flavors, and the perfect way to get more veggies onto the plate. Set up the lettuce cups and fillings like a taco bar and let everyone assemble their own for an epic #tacotuesday. And you can turn up the heat, if you like, by adding a little dab of your fave clean hot sauce.

SPICY MEDMEX TACO SAUCE

1 cup prepared tomato sauce

1 teaspoon red pepper flakes

½ teaspoon ground oregano

½ teaspoon ground cumin

½ teaspoon garlic powder

½ teaspoon sea salt

FILLING

2 tablespoons raw coconut oil or ghee, room temperature

½ yellow onion, finely chopped

4 fermented black garlic cloves or 2 regular garlic cloves (if you can't find black garlic), finely minced

1 pound ground turkey (or tempeh, for a vegan swap)

2 tablespoons minced fresh rosemary leaves

½ teaspoon sea salt

1 teaspoon freshly ground black pepper

2 cups finely chopped steamed cauliflower

TOPPING (OPTIONAL)

1 cup plain Greek yogurt (or coconut yogurt for a vegan swap)

2 tablespoons fresh lemon juice

24 whole Bibb or butter lettuce leaves

DIRECTIONS

1) MAKE THE SAUCE: In a medium saucepan, whisk together all the sauce ingredients and cook over medium heat, stirring occasionally, for 10 minutes.

2) MAKE THE FILLING: Meanwhile, in a large skillet, heat the raw coconut oil or ghee and sauté the onion over medium-low heat until translucent, about 5 minutes. Add the black garlic, ground turkey, rosemary, salt, and pepper. Cook, stirring, for 8 to 10 minutes, until the turkey is cooked through. Add cauliflower and cook for 2 minutes more.

3) MAKE THE TOPPING: In a small bowl, stir together the yogurt and lemon juice.

4) To assemble, spoon 2 tablespoons of the filling into each lettuce cup and top with 1 tablespoon of the sauce. Garnish with the topping, if desired, and serve.

POACHED EGG AND VEGGIE BREKKIE BOWL

This is my go-to way to start a power-packed day. When you break the silky yolks, they make the perfect sauce to toss with everything else. It's especially satisfying after an awesome workout. Lemme tell ya, you will not feel deprived with this bowl. It's sooo umami-yummy!

INGREDIENTS

½ cup ½-inch cubes sweet potato

2 tablespoons raw coconut oil or ghee (clarified butter), melted

½ teaspoon smoked sea salt, plus more as needed

2 cups ¼-inch cubes mixed nonstarchy veggies (zucchini, bell peppers, tomatoes, onions)

2 cups baby spinach

½ teaspoon chipotle chile flakes or red pepper flakes

1 teaspoon freshly ground black pepper, plus more as needed

2 tablespoons white vinegar

2 large eggs

½ avocado, cut into small chunks

DIRECTIONS

1) Preheat the oven to 400°F. Line a baking sheet with a silicone baking mat or aluminum foil.

2) In a small bowl, toss the sweet potato cubes with 1 tablespoon of the coconut oil and the smoked sea salt. Spread evenly over the prepared baking sheet and roast until fork-tender and slightly crisped, 15 to 20 minutes.

3) In a medium skillet, heat the remaining 1 tablespoon coconut oil over medium-high heat. Add the chopped veggies and cook, stirring, until just tender, 3 to 4 minutes. Add the spinach and cook until just wilted, about 1 minute. Season all the veggies with the chipotle flakes and black pepper. Remove from the heat.

4) In the meantime, fill a 2-quart saucepan with 2 inches of water and add the vinegar. Bring the water to a slow boil over high heat. Crack each egg separately into a strainer (this will make the eggs beautifully uniform) and carefully coax them into the water, keeping the yolk from breaking. With a long-handled spoon, gently swirl the water, creating a "whirlpool" to help keep the egg whites together. Set a timer for 5 minutes for soft-poached perfection. Remove the eggs from the water with a slotted spoon and place them on a plate lined with paper towels to absorb excess water.

5) To assemble each bowl, spoon the mixed veggies into half the bowl, the sweet potatoes into one-quarter, and the chopped avocado into the remaining quarter. Place one egg in the middle of each bowl. Finish the egg with a little smoked salt and black pepper and enjoy the yolky lusciousness.

HEIRLOOM TOMATO, CUCUMBER, FETA, AND DILL SALAD WITH PUMPKIN SEED OIL VINAIGRETTE

PUMPKIN SEED OIL VINAIGRETTE

2 tablespoons pumpkin seed oil (or extra-virgin olive or avocado oil, if pumpkin seed is unavailable)

1 tablespoon balsamic vinegar

2 teaspoons fresh lemon juice

1 teaspoon ground white pepper

½ teaspoon Himalayan pink salt

SALAD

1 cup chopped heirloom tomatoes

2 tablespoons ¼-inch cubes sheep's-or goat-milk feta cheese (or avocado, for vegan swap)

2 tablespoons ½-inch cubes cucumber

1 tablespoon thinly sliced red onion

2 teaspoons minced fresh dill leaves

DIRECTIONS

1) MAKE THE VINAIGRETTE: In a medium bowl, whisk together the pumpkin seed oil and vinegar until emulsified and well combined. Add the lemon juice, white pepper, and salt and whisk again.

2) Add the salad ingredients to the bowl with the vinaigrette and toss together until nicely coated. Serve with Thai Coconut Pumpkin Soup (page 128) for a well-rounded meal.

ZUCCHINI NOODLES WITH ROMESCO SAUCE

INGREDIENTS

1 tablespoon extra-virgin olive oil

4 zucchini, cut with a spiralizer into linguine-shaped noodles

1 cup Romesco Sauce (recipe follows)

1 tablespoon chopped fresh parsley

1 tablespoon grated pecorino cheese or other hard sheep's-milk cheese (optional but recommended)

DIRECTIONS

1) In a medium skillet, heat the olive oil over medium heat. Add the zucchini noodles and cook, stirring, for 2 to 3 minutes.

2) Transfer the zucchini noodles to a bowl and add the romesco sauce. Toss to thoroughly coat the noodles.

3) Finish with the parsley and cheese and twirl your zoodles with zeal!

Romesco Sauce

MAKES ¾ CUP OF SAUCE

The fanciest easy dish you'll ever make and want to eat by the spoonful. Use it on everything. 'Nuff said.

INGREDIENTS

1 large red bell pepper

1 cup grape tomatoes

2 garlic cloves

1 teaspoon smoked paprika

½ teaspoon ground cumin

¼ teaspoon sea salt

2 teaspoons extra-virgin olive oil

¼ cup pine nuts or blanched almonds

DIRECTIONS

1) Preheat the broiler or heat a grill to medium-high heat.

2) Broil or grill the bell pepper, tomatoes, and garlic until blistered with a bit of char and soft all the way through. Transfer the tomatoes and garlic to a food processor. Stem and seed the bell pepper and add it to the food processor as well.

2) Add the smoked paprika, cumin, salt, and olive oil and process until smooth. Add the pine nuts and pulse until combined but the nuts still have some texture.

3) Store the sauce in a sealed container in the refrigerator for up to 10 days. Toss it with veggie noodles or cooked proteins, or use it as a dressing.

GARLIC AND ROSEMARY BAKED OLIVES

INGREDIENTS

24 ounces mixed pitted olives (kalamata, Castelvetrano, Sicilian, colossal, and any other varieties)

2 tablespoons olive oil

3 garlic cloves, minced

1 tablespoon chopped fresh rosemary leaves

½ teaspoon lemon zest

1 tablespoon fresh lemon juice

½ teaspoon sea salt

½ teaspoon ground white pepper

DIRECTIONS

1) Preheat the oven to 400°F.

2) In a medium bowl, combine the olives, olive oil, garlic, rosemary, lemon zest, lemon juice, sea salt, and white pepper. Spread the olives over a rimmed baking sheet and roast for 15 to 20 minutes, until sizzling. Let cool.

3) Serve the olives or store in a sealed jar in the refrigerator for up to 21 days.

SUN-DRIED TOMATO, BASIL, AND WHITE BEAN DIP

INGREDIENTS

1 (15-ounce) can cannellini beans, drained and rinsed

2 garlic cloves, coarsely chopped

½ cup loosely packed fresh basil leaves

⅓ cup sun-dried tomatoes in oil, drained and coarsely chopped

1 tablespoon fresh lemon juice

¼ cup good-quality extra-virgin olive oil, plus more if needed

½ teaspoon sea salt

DIRECTIONS

1) Combine all the ingredients in a food processor and pulse until smooth, adding more olive oil if necessary until the desired consistency is reached.

2) Transfer to a serving bowl and serve with mixed veggies for snacking or use as a topping for convertible meal bowls.

LOW-SODIUM UMAMI BONE BROTH

My favorite way to make bone broth is in a slow cooker, but you can also do it in a pressure cooker. If you roast the veggies and bones first, it gives the broth an amazing, rich flavor. You will feel such a boost of energy from the natural collagen in the bones, too. You can use the same basic recipe for chicken bone broth. Feel free to add more veggies and turmeric or other spices to vary the flavor and make the broth more nutrient-dense. #betterthanbotox

INGREDIENTS

3 or 4 celery stalks, chopped into thirds

3 large carrots, chopped into 2-inch pieces

1 large red onion, quartered

2 garlic cloves, unpeeled

2 tablespoons ghee, melted

2½ to 3 pounds beef soup bones (see Note)

2 bay leaves

1 teaspoon sea salt

1 teaspoon freshly ground black pepper

3 tablespoons raw unfiltered apple cider vinegar

DIRECTIONS

1) Preheat the oven to 425°F.

2) In a large bowl, combine the celery, carrots, onion, and garlic and toss with the melted ghee. Put the bones in a roasting pan, add the vegetables, and spread everything into an even layer. Roast for 15 to 20 minutes, until the vegetables start to brown, taking care that nothing burns. Remove from the oven and transfer to a 6-quart slow cooker.

3) Add 12 cups water to the cooker (if your slow cooker is smaller, use less water). Cover and cook on Low for 12 hours.

While the broth is hot, strain out the solids and skim the fat from the surface, then allow to cool. Store the broth in airtight containers in the refrigerator. It may solidify a bit and become jelly-like—that's the collagen, the good stuff, so don't chuck it! When you reheat the broth, the collagen will liquefy—just give it a good stir to combine.

NOTE: For chicken bone broth, bring whole chicken to a boil, then reduce heat to a steady simmer for 1½ hours. Pick the meat off the bones and save it for another use and reserve the cooking liquid, straining out solids and fat from the surface. Place the bones with the veggies as you would the beef bones, and use the defatted chicken cooking liquid to finish the broth in the slow cooker.

REAL VITALITY TONIC

INGREDIENTS

1 cup hot water

1 tablespoon raw unfiltered apple cider vinegar

1 teaspoon fresh lemon juice

¼ teaspoon ground ginger

1 cinnamon stick

DIRECTIONS

Combine all the ingredients in a mug with 1 cup hot water and let steep for a few minutes. Sip after your first meal each day. Feel free to have a second cup later in the day, if you like, and save that cinnamon stick!

ROASTED SPICED ALMONDS

INGREDIENTS

2 tablespoons unsweetened cocoa powder

1 tablespoon ground cinnamon

1 teaspoon ground chili powder

1 teaspoon granulated stevia (use pure leaf granulated stevia and opt for organic when available)

½ teaspoon sea salt

2 cups whole raw almonds

1 tablespoon raw coconut oil

DIRECTIONS

1) Preheat the oven to 375°F.

2) Combine the cocoa powder, cinnamon, chili powder, stevia, and salt in a small bowl. Put the almonds in a medium bowl and rub them with the coconut oil. Add the spice mixture and toss until evenly coated. Arrange the almonds in a single layer on a rimmed baking sheet and bake for about 12 minutes, taking care not to burn the almonds and tossing as needed.

3) Remove from the oven and let cool. Store in parchment pouches at room temperature for up to 5 days.

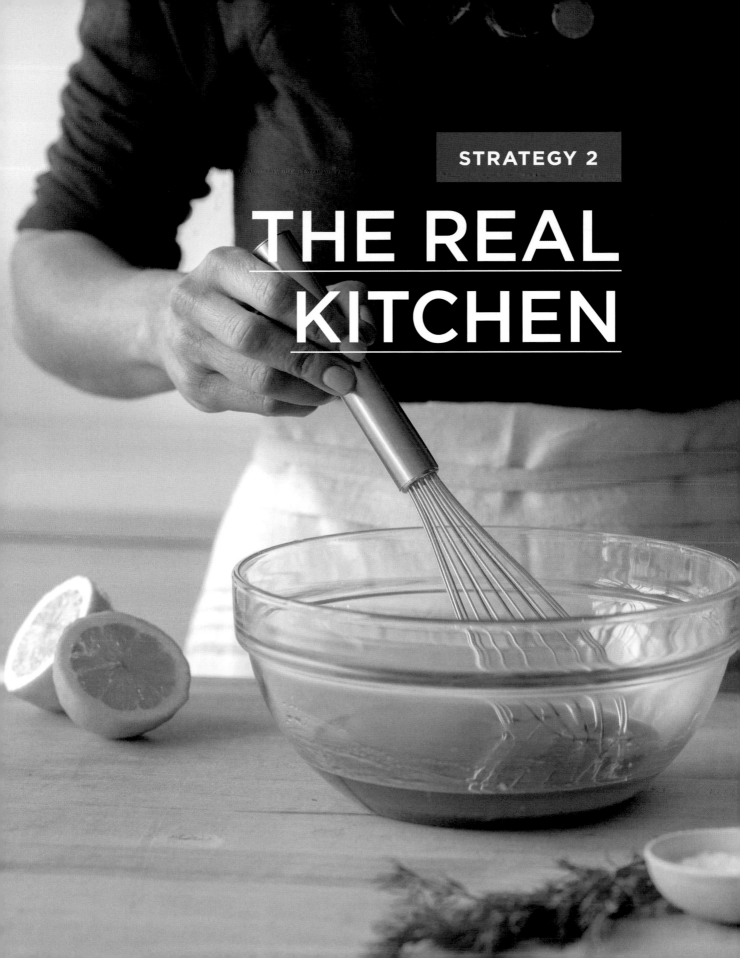

STRATEGY 2

THE REAL
KITCHEN

You know the scenario. It's 5:30 p.m., you're about to leave the office and thinking, *Hmmm, I wonder what I should make for dinner? Nah, I'll just hit the fast-food line.* Or you're starving, standing in front of your fridge with the door open, hoping the ingredients will get up, cut themselves for you, and shimmy their way into your salad bowl. . . . It's time to get real, my friend. We are going to make over your kitchen so you can consistently make the best choices for your body and your life.

If half your plate should be fresh produce, then half your fridge should be, too. Now that you've been through the taste bud reset, you're probably craving them as we speak! There's no room left for last season's crappy cookie dough with the sprinkles or the sugary cereal you've been hiding in the pantry and scooping up in handfuls when no one is looking. That would be an insult to your newly sculpted buds! In this strategy, we're going to surround you with color, brightness, freshness, and fun so you can pick and pair deliciously.

Make Room in Your Food Wardrobe

You know how you can always count on those jeans that make your butt look so good, the fitted shirt that flatters your biceps, and the belt and shoes that pull any look together? We'll take the same approach with food. We're going to build a great culinary wardrobe that mixes and matches beautifully, is full of color and gorgeous vibrancy, and has staples you can count on. We'll make it fresh and exciting from meal to meal, season to season, and with a variety of spice blends, marinades, seasonings, and toppings that cross cultures and continents and satisfy your need for variety, texture, and flavor. I've curated organizational tips for your fridge from my years of traveling and working in different kitchens, and I'll show you so it's a snap to follow.

Fresh, non-starchy vegetables dominate the plate, layered with clean proteins, single-ingredient grains, and quality fats. Having fresh food available gets you excited about your eating plan and stirs up your best results. Just like your wardrobe might be prêt-à-porter, the key is making these ingredients prêt-à-manger (ready to eat). All this involves is taking 10 minutes to wash, dry, and store your produce properly every week. On this program, you are going to be eating four or five times a day, and half of what you eat will be veggies, including tons o' greens at each meal, and low-glycemic-index fruits. Greens kick your metabolism and disease-fighting power into overdrive. They are what I call the turbo-chargers for that finely tuned body of yours.

In the *Eat Like You Give a Fork* program, you are making a commitment to fill your fridge with fresh veggies and fruits, storing your perishables so they hold up all week, "merchandising" them for maximum accessibility, flavor, and nutrient retention, and making them ready to eat. I'll also share easy ways to grow some of your own, so you get the freshest possible greens into your body every day. We'll also dive into our Meal Prep Power Hour later on in the "Convertible Meals" section, where we'll set a strategic plan for stocking basic pantry and fridge staples and create a playlist of favorite food groupings so you never have to wander aimlessly up and down the aisles of a grocery store again. You've got better things to do, hot stuff.

- Make Mixed Root Veggie chips (page 71).
- Make marinated Rockin' Raw Slaw (page 100) that holds up well in the fridge.
- Puree sweet potato, cauliflower, bell pepper, tomatoes, or greens to add to soups, sauces, and baked goods.
- Use veggies such as peppers (bell, Anaheim, jalapeño, serrano, etc.), zucchini, and Japanese eggplant as a vessel for stuffed meals. Add pureed or riced veggies like sweet potatoes, cauliflower, kohlrabi, and broccoli to the filling.
- Add Rainbow Veggie Quickles (page 76) to sandwiches and wraps. Cauliflower, carrots, celery, onions, and garlic are great options to add crunch and texture.

But It's Soooo Expensive

We all say we want to eat real, but I hear this excuse every day: "Eating cleaner is soooo expensive." Many people simply assume that eating right costs more. Is it true? According to the Bureau of Labor Statistics, as a country, we spend about a third less of our money on groceries than we did thirty years ago, and the cost of most foods has actually decreased. The way we spend our grocery money has also changed. We now spend so much more on processed food like frozen dinners, canned soups, and snacks—which I don't mind telling you are a minefield of sodium. By trimming your list down to the *Fork* essentials, you'll find you actually save a ton of dough.

Start by setting aside the $6 boxes of cereal, $5 coffee drinks, $4 bags of chips, and $3 energy bars, or, worse, the $50 restaurant tab for a few tacos!

Shopping for deals is so much easier when you have your staples in check. Look to international food stores and farmers' markets for some of the best prices on fresh seasonal produce, meats, fish, and grains. Farmers' markets are a great social experience for kids, and focus on locally produced foods. Many options are online now, so you can have your groceries delivered to your door and save your shopping list on the site so restocking is just a click away. Once you fill your fridge and pantry with what you'll need on a regular basis, keeping up with the fresh stuff and fill-ins becomes a habit.

If you have a plan and a list, you won't get distracted by the shiny, pretty bags, bottles, and boxes meant to seduce their way into your cart. Keep your eyes on the prize, folks!

"I'll just have one bite-size brownie," said no one ever.

The truth is, you either pay for nutritious whole foods as preemptive health care now, or pay doctor's bills later.

Pantry Raid

As you move away from preservatives and packaged foods manufactured to last for years and return to what we are meant to eat on a regular basis, you need to rethink your food storage. The task at hand is to reengineer your pantry so you have plenty of healthy, fresh, easy-to-grab food. This is a no-waste program that saves you time, money, and your sanity—and even your peels have a place on your plate.

Let's start with a little purging. If it's processed, bleached, contains high-fructose corn syrup, anything hydrogenated, the word *artificial*, trans fats, eight-syllable words, or anything on "The Steer-Clear List" (see below), it's outta there. Also look for sodium and sugar quantities. Your goal should be to keep your added sugar intake to less than 25 grams per day for the average woman and 30 to 35 grams for men; for sodium, limit your daily intake to 2,300 mg (1½ teaspoons).

The Steer-Clear List

Under no circumstances should you put the following ingredients in that precious bod of yours—or anyone else's, so don't donate them to the local food bank. If it's on the *Forkin'* "Steer-Clear" list, it's a goner. Just chalk it up to a learning moment, like when you decided acid-washed jeans and butt implants weren't the best ideas anymore.

1. Artificial colors: Food colorings are used to make food look more appealing or to replace colors lost in processing. However, don't let these colors deceive you. Artificial colorings are synthetic dyes that are often coal-tar derivatives. They may cause allergies, asthma, and hyperactivity, and are potentially carcinogenic. Where are they? In beverages, soda, gelatin-based desserts, pastries, farm-raised salmon, sausage, baked goods, and even fruits like green oranges sprayed with red dye to make them look ripe. Let Mother Nature do her job, for Pete's sake.

- Price-check items online. Scope out what fresh produce and meat is on sale. This is where you'll usually save the most money; stores always have featured specials.
- Shop with a list and stick to the plan. Avoid being seduced by the "sale items" you don't need.
- Buy in bulk or in larger sizes or containers, versus buying individual or single-serving items (yogurt, nuts, crackers, cheese, etc.), which are usually more expensive. Portion them yourself into reusable containers and snack bags.
- Shop the bulk bins for beans, rice, quinoa, bulgur, cereal, and nuts, since they are usually cheaper by the pound than prepackaged items and name brands.
- Avoid purchasing beverages such as bottled water and juice. It's much cheaper to get a water filter or pitcher, and way better for Mama Earth. Bottled juice can cost $4 to $5 per container. Make your own juice or super-fancy spa water (just add slices of lemon and cucumber, lime and fresh basil, or fresh mint and strawberries), and drink a ton more water every day.

2. Artificial preservatives (BHA, BHT, EDTA, sodium benzoate, etc.): You may see these ingredients in chips, fried snack foods, baked goods, carbonated drinks, cheese spreads, hummus, salsa, chewing gum, ice cream, breakfast cereals, and even cosmetics. These preservatives are actually synthetic petroleum-based and fat-soluble antioxidants (not the good kind!) used by manufacturers to prevent oxidation and retard rancidity. They can cause cancer, allergic reactions, and hyperactivity, and BHT may be toxic to the nervous system and the liver. Instead, look for cold-pressed virgin oils, which contain natural antioxidants such as vitamin E.

3. Nitrites and nitrates: Love your bacon in the morning and salami at lunchtime? Cured, preserved, and smoked meats are often saturated with nitrites and nitrates to preserve shelf life and give them a "healthy" pink hue. These two preservatives may prevent the growth of bacteria but can also transform into cancer-causing agents called nitrosamines in the stomach. They may also produce noticeable side effects like headaches, nausea, vomiting, and dizziness. Uncured meats don't use preservatives and are becoming much more widely available.

4. Monosodium glutamate (MSG): You may be happy that you're dining in restaurants that say "No MSG," but did you know that MSG lurks in all kinds of sauces used to prepare the foods you *thought* were MSG-free? There are also significant amounts in all kinds of snacks, seasonings, candy, infant formula, over-the-counter medications, and nutritional supplements. Instead, look for foods that are seasoned with natural flavors.

5. Trans fats: When you add hydrogen to vegetable oil, bad things happen. Fats turn into artery-cloggers that raise LDL ("bad") cholesterol levels and increase your risk of heart disease. Partially hydrogenated fats show up a lot in baked goods, fried foods, frostings, shortening, margarine, snack foods, coffee creamer, and refrigerated dough products. A big culprit is microwave popcorn. Why a manufacturer would take a vegetable and adulterate it like that, I will never understand. Bottom line: If you see the word *hydrogenated* anywhere on the ingredient panel, drop the package like it's hot and step away. Practice reading labels regularly, and before you know it, you'll become fluent in labelese.

Now, I know what you're thinking: But . . . *I LOVE those chocolate triple-stuffed cookies that rhyme with "sorry-os!" I'm just going to keep them on the top shelf—the just-in-case-I-have-a-bad-day shelf—and have just one only in an emergency.*

Relying on willpower isn't playing fair. You're stacking the odds against yourself, and babe, I don't want that for you. If you have a box of emergency cookies or an only-eat-them-when-there's-nothing-in-the-house bag of chips on the top shelf, they're gonna find a way into your mouth, and you know it's never just one. *Get them out of your home, pronto.* Once you purge the foods that don't fit you anymore, you'll have room for the new ingredients that make you look and feel like a god/dess.

Your Essential Refrigerator

Now that you've made room for the good stuff, it's time to build your wardrobe. This is the fun part, but I don't want you to be overwhelmed. You can do this in stages. Keep in mind that once you bring in the shelf-stable pantry items, they will last for quite a while. Buy perishable items based on seasons and sales, and plan ahead based on your *Forkin' Good* recipes for the week. Seasonal produce is the best way to eat, because you're enjoying foods at their brightest. You'll literally feel yourself vibrating with all that plant love coursing through your veins.

FRESH PRODUCE

Go seasonal as much as possible!

- [ ] Grapefruit
- [ ] Apples
- [ ] Pears
- [ ] Bananas
- [ ] Mixed berries
- [ ] Lemons/limes
- [ ] Fresh baby spinach, kale, and chard
- [ ] Romaine, red-/green-leaf, or butter lettuce
- [ ] Mixed salad greens (arugula, watercress, tatsoi, etc.) and microgreens
- [ ] Fresh mushrooms (cremini, shiitake, hen of woods, portobello, etc.)
- [ ] Broccoli
- [ ] Carrots
- [ ] Sweet potatoes
- [ ] Avocados
- [ ] Tomatoes
- [ ] Red onion
- [ ] Shallot
- [ ] Garlic
- [ ] Ginger
- [ ] Cucumber

ANIMAL/PLANT PROTEIN

- [ ] Salmon, mackerel, or sardines; tuna and other large fish 1x per week
- [ ] Chicken, turkey, Cornish game hen, duck
- [ ] Bison, lamb, beef, venison
- [ ] Organic tempeh
- [ ] Edamame
- [ ] Sea veggies (spirulina, blue-green algae, seaweed)

DELI/DAIRY

Not trying to be bougie, but when it comes to dairy and meat, try to pick grass-fed, free-range, wild-caught, organic, or sustainably raised when possible. These farming practices are better for the health of the animal, omit the use of excessive antibiotics, and produce a better balance of omega-3's versus the inflammatory omega-6's. We're getting you to enjoy more plant-based foods in this plan, and no dairy or meat at all on certain days, so you'll start to view it more as a condiment than the focus of the plate.

- [ ] Cage-free/organic eggs, whole eggs, and egg whites
- [ ] Plain Greek yogurt
- [ ] Fresh mozzarella (look for cherry-size balls labeled as "ciliegine")
- [ ] Raw goat's-milk or sheep's-milk cheese for grating
- [ ] Unsweetened coconut milk, almond milk, or sunflower milk (sunflower is nut-free)

- [ ] Sliced natural meats (uncured, nitrate-/nitrite-free)
- [ ] Ghee (clarified butter)

SUPER GLUTEN-FREE GRAINS

Make sure the label says "gluten-free" since many are processed in facilities that also process grains that contain gluten.

- [ ] Black and brown rice
- [ ] Freekeh
- [ ] Buckwheat
- [ ] Quinoa (any color)
- [ ] Kaniwa
- [ ] Teff
- [ ] Amaranth
- [ ] Millet
- [ ] Sorghum
- [ ] Quick-cooking oats
- [ ] Coconut flour, almond flour, oat flour, and/or good quality all-purpose gluten-free flour (avoid the white rice–based crap)

FREEZER SECTION

- [ ] Mixed berries (good for smoothies and purees)
- [ ] Organic edamame
- [ ] Veggie burgers

SHELF-STABLE

- [ ] Low-sodium beans (black beans, chickpeas, cannellini beans, or any variety you like)
- [ ] Low-sodium broth (chicken, beef, vegetable)
- [ ] Canned/pouch seafood: anchovies, albacore tuna, salmon, sardines
- [ ] Almond butter or sunflower butter (sunflower butter is nut-free)
- [ ] Peanut butter (powdered peanut butter is great for smoothies)
- [ ] Ground flaxseed and/or hemp seed
- [ ] Unsalted raw nuts (almonds, walnuts, cashews)
- [ ] Unsalted seeds (sunflower, pumpkin, sesame)
- [ ] Unsweetened and sulfite-free dried fruit (cranberries, figs, currants, etc.)
- [ ] Unsweetened shredded coconut
- [ ] Good-quality, low-to-no-sugar protein powder
- [ ] Dark chocolate (70% or more cacao)
- [ ] Unsweetened cocoa powder

CONDIMENTS/SAUCES

- [ ] Peanut butter or sunflower butter (sunflower butter is nut-free)
- [ ] Tahini (sesame paste)
- [ ] Raw coconut oil, ghee, and or grapeseed oil (for high-heat cooking)
- [ ] Extra-virgin olive oil
- [ ] Toasted sesame oil
- [ ] Nonstick olive or coconut oil cooking spray
- [ ] Balsamic vinegar
- [ ] Unfiltered apple cider vinegar
- [ ] Brown rice vinegar
- [ ] Coconut amino acids
- [ ] Whole leaf stevia or pure monkfruit extract, or a blend

SPICES/HERBS/CITRUS

- [ ] Fresh limes, lemons, and oranges
- [ ] Garlic
- [ ] Ginger
- [ ] Fresh and dried herbs (rosemary, basil, oregano, curry powder, paprika, cayenne pepper—experiment with what you like, since these are calorie-free flavors!)
- [ ] Sea salt and Himalayan pink salt
- [ ] Black pepper
- [ ] Mustard powder

Frigeratorganization

There's nothing more disheartening than reaching into the fridge to find the $7 organic berries are covered in moldy sweaters and the spinach has wilted and discharged green slime all over the floor of the crisper. Here's how to avoid this crime scene.

Check out my favorite fridge organizers in the "Must have tools of a fit foodie", just measure across your fridge to find ones that fit.

(See Mareya-Ibrahim.com)

You organize your closet so you can actually see the clothes you have in your wardrobe. You might even be one of those gold-star thinkers who groups outfits together, shoes neatly placed nearby in a perfect row, belts, hats, and purses at the ready for the accessorizing. Your refrigerator should look similar, more like a salad bar, with less emphasis on shelf-stable, processed foods in a box.

Gone are the days where poor produce sits in a plastic bag getting choked to death. By organizing your fridge like you would a great closet, you will turn it into a functional dining destination, and your family will know exactly what to grab and enjoy. If you prewash your fruit and veggies and put them in reusable BPA-free or glass containers, you and your family will be 100% more likely to eat more of them. Try it: Wash some strawberries or blackberries and put them out on the counter. They'll be gone in sixty seconds. Now leave them in the bag in your crisper and watch them grow mold in less than three days.

We throw away a lot of food. I mean TONS. Enough that according to the UN Environment Program, organic waste is the largest source of methane emissions. That largely comes from fresh food rotting in landfills. There's nothing that ticks me off more than spending hard-earned green on fresh food that goes bad the next day. Guess what? That never happens anymore because I can actually see what I have in my refrigerator, and it's prepped and ready for eatin'.

One-ingredient foods reign supreme. Pantry and fridge items should help you round out your balanced meals, including good sources of protein, complex carbohydrates, superfood add-ons (e.g., ground flaxseed, chia seeds, hemp oil, black seeds, turmeric root), spices, condiments, and high-quality oils that contribute essential fatty acids.

- **THE TOP SHELF:** Stock it with ingredients that help you create simple sauces and marinades, like low-sodium broths, stocks, veggie purees and nut milks.
- **FRIDGE BINS HOLD SMART SNACKING VEGGIES:** the hearty ones that hold up nicely and don't require much prep, like grape tomatoes, miniature bell peppers, Persian cucumbers, and radishes. Keep them in open containers at eye level so they're visible and ready to munch. These great raw veggie snacks will satisfy your need to crunch.
- The bottom shelf holds grab 'n' go meals, prepped and ready for you and your family. You can also have veggies and fruit that can be easily converted into meals, like Strawberry Coconut Nice Cream (page 217) or noodles made from squash or zucchini (page 39). More on this in "Convertible Meals."
- Fill the crisper drawer and baskets with prewashed greens, ready to throw into a smoothie, salad, soup, or entrée.
- Fill the meat/cheese drawer with precooked proteins and grains, including chicken, ground turkey, quinoa, farro, and such, all of which you will set up during our Meal-Prep Power Hour (see Convertible Meals, page 233).
- Stock the fridge door with sauces and toppings, pickles, etc. that will accessorize your meals with flavor.

Get Your Gear in Check

When my clients start their clean-eating journey, they sometimes feel overwhelmed at the sheer number of things they "need" to cook based on what they watch on TV and see in food stores. Or they're ready to get cooking, but then look at their kitchen and realize the pots and pans are peeling, the knives couldn't cut a piece of paper, and the broken blender is now a flowerpot.

Having the right stuff and being well-equipped in the kitchen will make your preparation much easier, more efficient, and way more enjoyable. But do you really need a tool to slice your eggs or pit your avocados? We'll take a quick tour of my essential kitchen tools and get your kitchen chef-ready for anything. In this case, less is definitely more. A few essential pieces of equipment will do a lot of the heavy lifting for you. These picks will also enable you to control portions and keep your cooking leaner and cleaner.

Think about your tools as enabling you to get more creative in the kitchen. Just like an artist, you'll have the ability to whip up meals with your signature touch. That's when you know you're getting comfortable and your cooking has moved well beyond a chore.

There are so many things I'd love to recommend, but I've whittled them down to a short list. These are *must-have* items to make your life easier. I do recommend some name-brand appliances, because I've tried so many varieties and found that certain ones work best. If you already have another brand, you don't need to run out and buy a new one. Make good use of what you've got.

HOW TO PREP PRODUCE FOR SUCCESS

I created the Eat Cleaner product line and system with you in mind and it's so easy-peasy, you can't muddle it up.

Take 5 minutes to wash fruit and veggies for the whole week with Eat Cleaner Fruit and Vegetable Wash and store them in see-through containers for easy snacking or to be used in soups, salads, sautés, and sandwiches. You'll be less likely to eat the stuff you're not supposed to, and the wash will help your produce last up to five times longer. That's free money.

DIRECTIONS
- Empty the Eat Cleaner produce wash packet into a gallon of cold water; mix well.
- Place the produce in Eat Cleaner mesh produce bags. Submerge the bags in the Eat Cleaner solution for 30 to 60 seconds; swish them through the solution.
- Remove the produce from the solution and drain excess water.
- Let the produce air-dry, then store in the fridge in a sealed container. Washing with Eat Cleaner will help your produce last up to 5x longer. Chop and chomp 'em up!

GR8 IDEAS FOR TURNING PANTRY STAPLES AND FRIDGE FARE INTO CLEANER FAST FOOD THAT'S GOOD FOR YOU

These snacks are a sure bet for avoiding a food emergency by stabilizing your blood sugar.

1. Stuff stalks of celery with Roasted Red Pepper Pesto (page 69).
2. Make veggie chips by slicing vegetables thin on a mandolin, spraying with nonstick cooking spray, and baking at 350°F until crisp (page 71).
3. Use pieces of napa cabbage or sheets of nori to roll up slices of turkey, ham, avocado, and cucumber or hummus so you can munch while you're rolling out the door.
4. Organic edamame and chickpeas can be baked and crisped when coated with a little nonstick cooking spray (see pages 26; 39; 69; 181); sprinkle with a dusting of chili powder or cumin.
5. Make a batch of The Best Kinda Date Balls (page 72) for a quick pick-me-up before and after workouts.
6. Core apples and slice them into ½-inch-thick rounds (like a donut), then top with nut butter and coconut flakes.
7. Grab some reusable cups or jars that'll fit in your car cup holder and fill them with carrot, celery, and jicama sticks. Put a couple tablespoons of any of my saucy dips and dressings (pages 26, 39, 69, 181) in the bottom.
8. Fill preportioned snack bags with raw almonds, dried coconut, goji berries, and almonds for the perfect energizer combo.

Prêt-à-Manger (Ready to Eat)

A funny thing happened on a plane heading back from New York City. I was waiting to use the restroom when a woman behind me asked if I was cold. She was wearing a full-length wool coat, a sweater, and a turtleneck. I was in a thin, long-sleeved shirt. When I replied, "No, I'm very comfortable," she went on about how freezing cold the plane was.

I asked her when she had eaten last, and she curtly replied that she had had "a lot" to eat right before getting on the plane. Curious, I asked her what "a lot" meant, as she was very petite, like me. I mentioned that when your blood sugar drops, you sometimes feel cold. She blasted back that she was a cancer doctor and that it had nothing to do with digestion.

A nutrition challenge? In my head I was thinking, *Game on like Donkey Kong, this is MY house* . . . but, of course, I took this as an opportunity to politely delve further into a discussion. I may have permanently scarred my tongue with how many times I had to bite it. Here's a recap of our conversation:

Doctor: Food has nothing to do with feeling warm.

Me: But, Doctor, you know that digestion causes your body to burn calories, creating heat through energy.

Doctor: Whenever I eat, I always feel very sleepy. Eating makes me feel tired. I'm very hypoglycemic.

Me: All the more reason to eat the right combination of foods more frequently. If you did, you would feel more energetic. What do you usually eat?

Doctor: Oh, I only eat protein. Very little carbs.

Me: Doctor, that may be the problem. If you're not eating carbs, your body will have a hard time metabolizing the protein, and you will not have energy quickly available to burn. Perhaps you should try eating more fresh vegetables with your protein and essential fatty acids, and eat every three to four hours. I could suggest a good meal plan if you'd like to try it.

I wanted to say, "Eat four or five clean meals a day and call me in the morning," but then it was my turn to go to the bathroom. With all due respect, I'm not saying I know more than a doctor, but if eating makes you feel tired and sluggish, it's probably time to reevaluate what's on your plate.

> Clean foods + smaller portions = higher metabolism

Not eating frequently enough triggers a signal that your body thinks it's starving, which makes it hold on to fat. While you can stoke your body's natural fire by leading with a half plate of nonstarchy veggies and layering up from there, the real goal is to get a complete balance of amino acids into every meal.

I want you to throw the idea of three square meals a day out the window. Buh-bye! This may be one of the most important shifts in thinking when it comes to adopting my way of eating. Eating smaller meals with the right balance of lean protein, slow-burning carbs, and essential fats every three to four hours with fat fillers in between is the most effective way to force your body to burn fat, stave off hunger, and stabilize blood sugar.

You will *not* gain weight, because you're eating the right nutrients for your body and allowing your metabolism to kick into high gear without letting your hormones get in the way. You won't feel famished because you've waited too long to eat. You never say, "I'm so full I can't move." And with this plan you just won't let yourself get into the food 911 zone.

Gone are the days when you wandered through the grocery aisles wondering what to prepare. When you've got a plan, you're always food-dressed for success. Our Sample Meal Plan (page 68) will give you the flexibility of being able to mix and match ingredients, sauces, and seasonings to get the variety you desire. That culinary wardrobe will always be there for you.

THE MUST-HAVE TOOLS TO EAT LIKE YOU GIVE A FORK

Here's my must-have list of kitchen tools, but check out the links for specific products at eatcleaner.com/product-category/chef-mareya-recommends and make your stock-up process a lot less painful:

- Measuring cups and spoons
- Clear BPA-free square or rectangular reusable containers to store food in various sizes
- Insulated cooler to transport meals
- Large colander to wash produce
- Fine mesh strainer to clean small single-ingredient grains and strain sauces and broths
- 3 thick plastic cutting boards: 1 for produce, 1 for meats/fish, 1 for everything else
- Veggie peeler to make ribbons out of zucchini, carrots, squash, etc.
- Microplane to grate nutmeg, dark chocolate, and citrus zest
- Food processor to make sauces, chop veggies, and process grains
- High-powered blender to make smoothies and sauces
- Chef's knife and paring knives (make sure they're sharp)
- Small and medium ice cream scoop to form meatballs, Fit Bites, and portion-controlled desserts
- Baking dishes with lids in various sizes to make storage and cleanup easier
- Veggie steamer
- Teflon-free nonstick pans: grill pan, crepe pan, large stockpot, large nonstick skillet
- Rice cooker to easily cook grains and stuffed peppers perfectly
- Slow cooker to cook fit meals while you're away from home
- Immersion blender to puree foods right in the pot or bowl

SAMPLE MEAL PLAN (ALL DISHES ARE 1 SERVING, UNLESS NOTED OTHERWISE)

	SUNDAY	MONDAY	TUESDAY	WEDNESDAY	THURSDAY	FRIDAY	SATURDAY
BREAKFAST	Spinach Mushroom Frittata Cups Melon fruit salad	Pumpkin Spice Protein Smoothie	Pitaya Fruit Bowl	Quinoa Breakfast Bake	Pitaya Fruit Bowl	Quinoa Breakfast Bake	Pumpkin Spice Protein Smoothie
SNACK	You Glow Smoothie	Spinach Mushroom Frittata Cup	Fit Bites (2)	Chocolate Coco Nutter w/ Pears	Fit Bites (2)	You Glow Smoothie	Spinach Mushroom Frittata Cup
LUNCH	Spaghetti Squash Pad Thai Green Salad	Chicken Sausage Spelt Skillet Zucchini Carpaccio	Kaniwa and Fresh Herb Tabbouli Blender Gazpacho	Down & Dirty Green Curry Black or Brown Rice	Kaniwa and Fresh Herb Tabbouli Blender Gazpacho	Braised Celery Puttanesca Zucchini Carpaccio	Moroccan Spice Chicken Legs Molokhiya Soup
SNACK	Chocolate Coconutter w/ Sliced Pears	Fit Bites (2)	Crunch Chickpeas (2)	You Glow Smoothie	Crunch Chickpeas (2)	You Glow Smoothie	Pitaya Fruit Bowl
DINNER	Chicken Sausage Spelt Skillet Green Salad	Down & Dirty Green Curry Black or Brown Rice	Wild Mushroom Amaranth & Colorful Cauliflower Blender Gazpacho	Moroccan Spice Chicken Legs Molokhiya Soup Tri-Colored Quinoa	Braised Celery Puttanesca Zucchini Carpaccio	Kofta Bison Burger All the Fixins'	Spaghetti Squash Pad Thai Thai Coconut Soup
10% EXTRA	No Bake Oatmeal Peanut Butter Chocolate Chip Cookies					Tahini Marble Fudge	Strawberry Coconut Nice Cream
	1488 Calories; 134 Protein; 168 Carbs, 50 Dietary; 40 Fat; 6 Sat; 322 Cholest; 1398 Sodium	1584 Calories; 142 Protein; 145 Carbs, 48 Dietary; 60 Fat; 10 Sat; 188 Cholest; 1504 Sodium	1624 Calories; 136 Protein; 158 Carbs, 49 Dietary; 49 Sugars; 49 Dietary; 108 Est Net; 59 Fat; 210 Cholest; 1384 Sodium	1527 Calories; 142 Protein; 180 Carbs, 52 Dietary; 37 Fat; 4 Sat; 151 Cholest; 623 Sodium	1521 Calories; 116 Protein; 184 Carbs, 37 Dietary; 52 Fat; 11 Sat; 362 Cholest; 885 Sodium	1573 Calories; 132 Protein; 172 Carbs, 51 Dietary; 49 Fat; 8 Sat; 136 Cholest; 1284 Sodium	1507 Calories; 150 Protein; 151 Carbs, 47 Dietary; 44 Fat; 6 Sat; 162 Cholest; 1109 Sodium

MAKES 4 SERVINGS

ROASTED RED PEPPER PESTO

INGREDIENTS

1 cup packed fresh basil

1 teaspoon raw unfiltered apple cider vinegar

4 ounces jarred roasted red peppers, drained

½ teaspoon lemon zest

Juice of 1 lemon

2 tablespoons pine nuts

1 garlic clove

½ teaspoon sea salt

½ teaspoon freshly ground black pepper

2 tablespoons extra-virgin olive oil

DIRECTIONS

1) In a food processor, combine all the ingredients except the olive oil and pulse until smooth.

2) With the motor running, slowly add the olive oil through the feed tube and process until creamy, about 30 seconds.

3) Toss with spiralized squash noodles, fresh veggies, or grilled chicken and seafood. Store extra pesto in an airtight glass jar for up 14 days.

MAKES 4 CUPS (8 HALF-CUP SERVINGS)

MIXED ROOT VEGGIE CHIPS

Talk about a fun way to eat the rainbow! You can use big carrots, beets, purple sweet potatoes, and parsnips to get a whole array of color on your plate. The best way to get these veggie chips uber thin is by using a mandoline slicer, but a *strong* word of caution: Please be careful. Use the cutting guard and don't multitask while you're slicing. Keep your focus on the very sharp blade in front of you. I don't want you making a finger chip. You can also use the slicing attachment on your food processor, or a special chopping tool.

INGREDIENTS

6 medium assorted root veggies (carrots, golden beets, purple beets, sweet potatoes, parsnips, turnips), sliced paper-thin on a mandoline (4 cups total)

3 tablespoons extra-virgin olive oil

1 tablespoon ground cumin or turmeric

Himalayan pink salt

DIRECTIONS

1) Preheat the oven to 325°F. Line a large baking sheet with parchment paper or a silicone baking mat.

2) In a gallon-sized container, toss together the sliced veggies, olive oil, and cumin, rubbing the oil over all the surfaces to coat.

3) Arrange the veggies in a single layer on the prepared baking sheet and sprinkle with salt. Bake until crispy, 25 to 30 minutes. Remove from the oven and let cool for 5 to 10 minutes before enjoying.

THE BEST KINDA DATE BALLS

What's the best kind of date? The one you can eat.

INGREDIENTS

1 cup dried dates, pitted and chopped

½ cup raw almonds

½ cup chopped walnuts

½ cup ground flaxseed

1 scoop collagen protein powder (or plant-based protein, for a vegan swap)

¼ cup plus 2 tablespoons unsweetened shredded coconut

FLAVORING OPTIONS

**Matcha Tea Date Balls:
Add ½ teaspoon fine matcha tea powder to mixture**

Pea-nutty Date Balls:
Add 2 tablespoons chopped peanuts + 1 teaspoon ground cinnamon to mixture

DIRECTIONS

1) In a food processor, combine the dates, almonds, walnuts, ground flaxseed, protein powder, ¼ cup of the coconut, the flavoring ingredients of your choice, and 2 teaspoons water and pulse until a dough is formed. Add another teaspoon or two of water if needed for the mixture to hold together.

2) Spread the remaining 2 tablespoons coconut over a small plate. Roll the dough into twelve 1-ounce balls, then roll each in the coconut to coat, setting the balls on a large plate as you go.

3) Freeze the balls for 30 minutes in a sealed container to firm up, and to store any uneaten balls for indulging when your heart desires.

CRUNCHY FLAMIN' CHICKPEAS

Forget about flaming snacks that stain your hands permanently. These crunchy legumes give your metabolism a nice boost with a clean snack that satisfies your need to crunch—and no Day-Glo orange dust.

INGREDIENTS

4 cups canned chickpeas, drained, rinsed, and patted dry

2 teaspoons raw coconut oil, melted

2 teaspoons ground cumin

1 teaspoon chili powder

1 teaspoon cayenne pepper

½ teaspoon smoked sea salt

DIRECTIONS

1) Preheat the oven to 400°F and position a rack in the middle of the oven. Line a rimmed baking sheet with a silicone baking mat or parchment paper.

2) In a large bowl, combine all the ingredients and toss until the chickpeas are evenly coated.

3) Spread the chickpeas in an even layer over the prepared baking sheet and bake for 40 minutes. Remove from the oven and let cool for 30 minutes (the longer they cool, the crispier they'll get). These don't store for long without getting soggy, but wrapped up tightly in a cone of parchment paper, they'll last for 3 to 4 days.

MAKES 10 TO 12 SERVINGS

RAINBOW VEGGIE QUICKLES

These quick-pickled veggies that I affectionately call quickles are ready to eat in less than an hour but get better with time. Pickled veggies are a big part of my upbringing, and one of my favorite things to keep in the fridge to complement just about every meal. The addition of sour pickled prebiotic probiotic goodness will really start to shift your gut health, and the multicolored veggies are the best way to make sure you're eating the rainbow. Don't be surprised if you see a unicorn or two.

QUICKLE JUICE

3 cups raw unfiltered apple cider vinegar

1 tablespoon whole black peppercorns

2 tablespoons fresh dill leaves

2 teaspoons sea salt

1 teaspoon granulated stevia

VEGETABLES

1 onion, quartered and thinly sliced

2 cups small cauliflower florets (use a mix of purple and green cauliflower for fun color)

2 carrots, sliced on a mandoline or cut into ¼-inch-thick slices with a knife

1 cup small-diced yellow or red beets

DIRECTIONS

1) MAKE THE QUICKLE LIQUID: In a medium saucepan, combine all the quickle liquid ingredients with 1 cup water and bring to a boil.

2) Place each vegetable in a glass jar with a lid. Pour enough quickle liquid into each jar to cover the vegetables completely. Let cool to room temperature before sealing the jars.

3) Store the quickles in the refrigerator for up to 2 months. Make sure to keep the jars sealed airtight for maximum freshness, and use a clean fork or spoon when removing quickles from the jars.

ZUCCHINI CARPACCIO AND ARUGULA STACK

INGREDIENTS

4 zucchini, sliced into thin sheets with a mandoline or veggie peeler

¼ cup plus 2 tablespoons The Real Dish Dressing (page 26)

1 cup arugula

¼ cup grape tomatoes, sliced

¼ cup grated Pecorino cheese

Freshly ground black pepper

DIRECTIONS

1) Put the zucchini slices in a shallow dish and pour over ¼ cup of the dressing. Marinate for at least 30 minutes and up to 2 hours.

2) On a large plate, arrange a layer of the zucchini strips, then add a layer of strips perpendicular to the first, for a fun grid pattern.

3) In a small bowl, toss the arugula and tomatoes with the remaining 2 tablespoons dressing.

4) Arrange the arugula and tomatoes over the zucchini carpaccio and finish with the pecorino and some freshly ground black pepper.

THE BEST BLENDER GAZPACHO

When it's too hot to eat soup or you want to sip on something more savory than a smoothie, gazpacho is a go-to source of real nutrition in a glass. It's all veggies, and goes down like buttah and you get the bennies of everything being raw. Making it in the blender means it's ready in no time flat, and everybody's got time for that.

INGREDIENTS

2 cups low-sodium vegetable broth

1 (28-ounce) can whole peeled tomatoes

3 Persian cucumbers, cut into chunks

1 red or yellow bell pepper, top cut off, cut into quarters

1 medium Vidalia (sweet) onion, quartered

4 fermented black garlic cloves

3 tablespoons extra-virgin olive oil

2 tablespoons balsamic vinegar

1½ teaspoons smoked paprika

1 teaspoon freshly ground black pepper

1 teaspoon kosher salt

1 teaspoon ground cumin

Diced avocado, for serving (optional)

Diced onions, for serving (optional)

DIRECTIONS

1) Pour the broth into a high-speed blender, then add the tomatoes and pulse until smooth. Pour half the mixture into a large pitcher and set aside.

2) Add the cucumbers, bell pepper, onion, and black garlic to the blender and pulse until smooth. Add a little more of the tomato-broth mixture from the pitcher, if needed, to help break down the vegetables.

3) Pour the puree into the pitcher with the tomato-broth mixture and whisk in the olive oil, vinegar, paprika, black pepper, salt, and cumin until well combined.

4) Cover and refrigerate for at least 1 hour to get the gazpacho nice and chilled before serving.

5) Pour the gazpacho into bowls and top with diced avo and onions, if desired, for a little extra somethin' somethin'.

GUACAMOLE BELL PEPPER NACHOS

BEST GUAC EVAH

3 ripe avocados

1 teaspoon grated lime zest

Juice of 2 limes

1 small red onion, finely minced

2 garlic cloves, minced

2 tablespoons minced fresh cilantro

½ teaspoon ground white pepper

½ teaspoon Himalayan pink salt

½ teaspoon ground cumin

¼ teaspoon cayenne pepper

3 bell or pasilla peppers, sliced lengthwise into 2-inch "tortilla chip" shapes, for serving

DIRECTIONS

1) MAKE THE GUAC: Halve and pit the avocados and scoop the flesh into a medium bowl. Add the lime zest and lime juice and use the bottom of a mason jar, sturdy-bottomed glass, or mortar and pestle to smash the avocado flesh until smooth. This allows you to keep some texture without making a puree.

2) Add the onion, garlic, cilantro, white pepper, salt, cumin, and cayenne and mix with a fork to combine.

3) Spoon the guac into a serving bowl and serve with the bell pepper "chips" for dipping, or spoon the guacamole into the peppers for a great appetizer.

OVERSTUFFED SWEET POTATOES WITH CHIPOTLE-LIME YOGURT

SWEET POTATOES

4 small to medium sweet potatoes, or 2 large sweet potatoes cut in half

2 tablespoons ghee (clarified butter) or raw coconut oil

Sea salt and freshly ground black pepper

CHIPOTLE-LIME YOGURT

1 cup plain Greek yogurt

½ teaspoon dried chipotle chile powder

1 tablespoon fresh lime juice

TOPPINGS

1 cup cooked or canned black beans (drained and rinsed, if canned)

1 avocado, cubed

2 tablespoons chopped fresh cilantro

2 teaspoons chopped fresh chives

1 tablespoon hemp hearts (optional)

Freshly ground black pepper

DIRECTIONS

1) Preheat the oven to 425°F. Line a rimmed baking sheet with aluminum foil.

2) Put the sweet potatoes on the prepared baking sheet and roast until fork-tender, about 45 minutes. Remove from the oven.

3) Slice the potatoes lengthwise down the center and rake fork through to "fluff up" the soft flesh. Work 1 teaspoon of the ghee and a light sprinkle of salt and pepper into each potato.

4) MAKE THE CHIPOTLE-LIME YOGURT: Combine all the chipotle-lime yogurt ingredients in a small bowl and stir well.

5) Put each sweet potato on a serving plate and top with ¼ cup of the black beans each. Top with 1 tablespoon of the cubed avocado, 1½ teaspoons of the parsley, ½ teaspoon of the chives, and a drizzle of the chipotle-lime yogurt. Garnish with a sprinkle of hemp hearts, if desired, and another grind of black pepper. #nomnom

SPAGHETTI SQUASH PAD THAI

INGREDIENTS

1 (3- to 4-pound) spaghetti squash, top trimmed, halved lengthwise, and seeded

Nonstick olive or coconut oil cooking spray

2 tablespoons raw coconut oil

1 pound 16-20 ct. raw shrimp, peeled and deveined

3 garlic cloves, minced

Juice of 2 limes

3 tablespoons coconut amino acids

1 tablespoon granulated stevia or monkfruit sweetener

1 tablespoon red chile paste

2 large eggs, lightly beaten

TOPPINGS

1 cup shredded carrots

4 scallions, sliced

¼ cup roasted peanuts, chopped

¼ cup fresh cilantro, chopped

DIRECTIONS

1) Preheat the oven to 425°F. Line a rimmed baking sheet with a silicone baking mat or parchment paper.

2) Mist the cut sides of the squash with cooking spray and place on the prepared baking sheet. Roast for 30 to 40 minutes, until the squash's flesh is tender and can easily be removed from the skin with a fork. Let the squash cool slightly, then scrape the flesh into spaghetti-like strands with a fork and transfer to a bowl. Set the scraped shells aside.

3) In the meantime, in a large skillet, melt 1 tablespoon of the coconut oil over medium heat. Add the shrimp and cook until pink and opaque on each side, about 2 minutes. Remove from the heat and set aside.

4) In a small bowl, whisk together the garlic, lime juice, amino acids, stevia, and red chile paste.

5) Return the skillet to medium-high heat and melt the remaining 1 tablespoon coconut oil. Add the squash and pour the garlic lime juice mixture over the top. Toss thoroughly to evenly coat the squash. Add the beaten egg and quickly cook for 2 minutes.

6) Top with the shrimp, carrots, scallions, peanuts, and cilantro, and serve.

DOWN-AND-DIRTY GREEN CURRY

It really doesn't matter what you put in the curry, because the sauce just makes everything taste good. You can go crazy with the veggies, chicken, seafood, or tempeh with this base recipe that you can customize. The beautiful part is, curry becomes so unintimidating when you see just how easy and quick this is to pull together.

INGREDIENTS

1 tablespoon raw coconut oil

¼ cup green curry paste (I use Thai Kitchen)

¼ cup red onion, diced into rings then cut in half

1¼ to 1½ pounds chicken breasts (see Notes), cleaned and cut into bite-size cubes

1 cup low-sodium vegetable broth

1 (14-ounce) can unsweetened full-fat coconut milk

2 cups mixed vegetables (see Notes)

½ teaspoon kosher salt

½ teaspoon ground white pepper

Cooked brown or black rice, for serving

DIRECTIONS

1) In a large heavy-bottomed skillet, melt the coconut oil over medium heat. Add the curry paste and cook until fragrant, about 2 minutes. Add the onion and cook, stirring, until translucent, 2 to 3 minutes.

2) Add the chicken and cook, stirring, for 2 to 3 minutes. Add the broth and coconut milk and bring the mixture to a boil. Reduce the heat to medium and add the vegetables. Season the mixture with the salt and white pepper. Cook for 10 minutes, or until chicken is cooked through and the sauce has reduced by at least one-third.

3) Ladle the curry over individual bowls of brown or black rice and bask in the glow of the heat.

NOTES: You could also use shrimp or pork loin in place of the chicken. For a vegetarian curry, omit the chicken and double up on the mixed veggies or use organic tempeh.

For the mixed veggies, try a combination of at least two of the following:
• Bell pepper, halved crosswise and sliced into ½-inch-thick strips
• Japanese eggplant, cut into ½-inch cubes
• Carrots, diced
• Japanese yams, diced
• Snap peas

BAKED WILD SOLE AND VEGGIES IN PARCHMENT

INGREDIENTS

4 ounces cremini (baby bella) mushrooms, thinly sliced

1 red onion, thinly sliced

½ pound Brussels sprouts (purple, if you can find them), shredded or finely chopped

1 cup grape tomatoes, halved

½ cup kalamata olives, pitted

½ teaspoon sea salt

1 teaspoon freshly ground black pepper

¼ cup dry white wine

2 tablespoons extra-virgin olive oil

Juice of ½ lemon

2 teaspoons ground cumin

1 teaspoon ground coriander

4 (4- to 6-ounce) wild-caught sole or sustainable white-fleshed fish fillets

1 lemon, cut into wedges to serve on the side

DIRECTIONS

1) Preheat the oven to 375°F. Cut four 12x16-inch rectangles of parchment paper. Fold each in half lengthwise to make four 12x8-inch rectangles, then open them back up.

2) In a large bowl, combine the mushrooms, onion, Brussels sprouts, tomatoes, and olives and season with the salt and pepper. Divide the vegetables evenly among the parchment rectangles, piling them on one half of the paper, close to the crease.

3) In a small bowl, whisk together white wine, olive oil, lemon juice, ground cumin, and ground coriander. Lay one portion of fish onto each bed of vegetables and spoon mixture over fish and veggies. Carefully seal the parchment by crimping and folding the edges to form a pouch shaped like a half-moon.

4) Set the parchment pouches on a baking sheet and bake until the veggies are cooked through and the fish flakes apart when you prod it with your finger (you'll need to open one of the pouches a little by unfolding the edge to check), 10 to 12 minutes.

5) Serve the pouches on individual plates, or transfer the contents to plates (be careful, as the steam inside will be hot). Serve with remaining lemon wedges.

GET UP
ON GREENS

If your introduction to greens was eating raw, undressed kale, I'm so, so sorry. Can we start over?

I grew up watching *Popeye*, so the association of greens with strength has always been parked in my brain ("I'm strong to the finish, 'cuz I eats me spinach, I'm Popeye the Sailor Man!"). The truth is, the top ten most nutrient-dense foods on the planet are greens—meaning calorie for calorie, you get the most nutritional bang for your calorie buck when you eat them. They will change your palate, your energy, your vitality, and your waistline for the better. I'm gonna go out on a limb and say they will turn back the clock. I swear, when I started filling up on greens and prioritizing them on my plate, I stopped seeing gray hairs pop up. No joke. Now, I'm not guaranteeing that outcome, but premature graying runs in my family, and at the time of this book's publication, I haven't had to cover them yet. You will probably get a lot of people saying, "Um, have you had some work done? You look AH-MAYYYYY-ZING." And you'll say, "Um, no, RUDE. And by the way, thanks."

There's a scientific reason for this. Greens are filled with magnesium, which helps delay mitochondrial decay, the decay of the cell's brain. When your cells age, you age. When your cells are fed right, they're stayin' alive on the dance floor. Greens are also an awesome source of B vitamins, which can ward off stress, heart disease, and dementia, and vitamin K, which builds calcium in your bones. They also bring omega-3 fatty acids to the table. The darker the greens, the sweeter the honey, know what I mean? Not to mention, greens are jam-packed with antioxidants, which, like their name says, prevent oxidation. Everything we do to prevent oxidation in our bodies helps to keep us healthy and ward off disease, cell degeneration, and cell death. Imagine you've got the big guns out holding those free radicals at bay. Protect those cells with heavy-duty bulletproof vests.

Never have there been so many options that deliver a knockout punch of phytonutrients to boost your cardiovascular, metabolic, and brain health while literally turning back the clock on aging.

With this program, we're going to get up on greens. That's street lingo for "we're going to get funky with 'em," make them our bae, our go-to, our nugs, because they are everything. Unlike any other veg, they're going to reshape your palate to appreciate more of the stuff you want to eat on the regular. Since you've just learned how to flex your flabby taste buds, this is the ideal place to start crushing on cabbage, chard, kale, chicory, collards, and all your other new green bffs. We're talking way beyond salads here, friends. Never have there been so many options that deliver a knockout punch of phytonutrients to boost your cardiovascular, metabolic, and brain health while literally turning back the clock on aging.

ADDITIONAL BENNIES OF GREENS

- Help with weight management
- Reduce the risk of cancer and heart disease
- Low in calories
- Low in fat
- High in fiber
- Rich in folic acid, vitamin C, potassium, and magnesium, as well as phytochemicals (aka Disease Destroyers) such as lutein, beta-cryptoxanthin, zeaxanthin, and beta-carotene, which helps support a strong immune system
- Low glycemic index
- Loaded with carotenoids, flavonoids, and other powerful antioxidants
- Cabbage, cauliflower, Brussels sprouts, and broccoli: Rich in indoles and isothiocyanates, which help protect against different cancers including colon and breast cancer

Greens are your new friends with bennies, so knowing how to best use them will change your life. There is just one hook: To bring out the best in greens, you have to work with their personality. Some are easygoing and don't need a lot of work. Others need a little more attention. Remind you of anyone you know?

You can pretty much break up the greens family into three categories.

1. Mild Greens: romaine lettuce, red- and green-leaf lettuce, butter lettuce, watercress, Bibb lettuce, arugula (rocket), endive, baby kale, baby spinach, microgreens

Mild greens are your "fun friends." They're low-maintenance and easy to work with, like your go-to black dress or those jeans that fit your butt so perfectly. Enjoy salad greens raw, crisp, and cold, and dress them up with a little oil and vinegar, The *Real Dish* Dressing (page 26), or any one of the yummy sauces in this book (pages 39, 69, 181). For smoothies, baby kale and spinach work best.

2. Rich Greens: tuscan kale (lacinato or dinosaur kale), curly kale, Swiss chard, broccoli, celery and greens, escarole, radicchio, green cabbage, napa cabbage, broccoli rabe (rapini), bok choy

Although you can enjoy rich greens raw, they usually need a little massaging. Balance them out with fat and acid: Coconut oil, ghee, avocado oil, extra-virgin olive oil, amino acids, vinegar, and citrus help round them out and soften them up. Rub the leaves with a fat-acid combo—and when I say "rub," I mean really work it in—and let them marinate for a few hours. Watch their texture and flavor transform. Rich greens also hold up well to cooking, which can also mellow their slight bitterness.

3. Hearty Greens: dandelion greens, collard greens, turnip greens, mustard greens

These greens can be pretty assertive and a little rough around the edges, but they're so worth the love and attention. They need heat to mellow them out, and love a good sauté with some denser fat, like coconut oil or avocado oil, and a nice amino-umami combo to bring out the best in their flavor profiles. They also love a good comingling with garlic, onions, and shallots or a dip into a coconut milk–based sauce.

My go-to greens are baby spinach, Tuscan kale (lacinato or dinosaur kale), baby kale, collards, mustard, beet, broccoli, broccoli rabe (rapini), Brussels sprouts, arugula, Swiss chard, watercress, butter lettuce, baby spinach, tatsoi, romaine lettuce, microgreens (all types), endive, radicchio, and dandelion greens. Now make a list of your faves and put them at the top of your shopping list. When you're thinking about food choices, one or more of these should make an appearance in every meal. #greengoalz

I SEA WEED

A whole new wave of greens has taken over, and they aren't lit up but they might be inhaled. The weed of the sea goes way beyond sushi. Nori, hijiki, kombu, and kelp are just a few of the common names. Use as seasoned snacking strips, in salads, and wraps, and as seasonings for rice. The beauty of sea veggies is that they offer a multitude of minerals, including iron, magnesium, calcium, and clean iodine to help regulate hormone balance, metabolize vitamin C supplies, and boost your body's ability to fight oxidative stress. They'll also help turbocharge your taste buds, so for all you mermaids and mermen, roll 'em, stack 'em, and shred 'em up! And here's a fun little hack: Want to take the gas out of beans? Throw some kombu into your pot of beans while cooking, and boom—no gassy poos.

Flavors that complement an array of greens include:
- Fat (olive oil, avocado oil, whole avocado, coconut oil, ghee)
- Fruit Acid (zest and juice of lemon, lime, grapefruit, orange, mandarin)
- Vinegar (raw unfiltered apple cider vinegar, red/white wine vinegar, rice vinegar, balsamic vinegar, coconut vinegar)
- Amino acids (coconut aminos, soy-based aminos)
- Garlic (fermented black garlic, white garlic, granulated garlic, garlic powder)
- Onions (shallots, leeks, scallions, red onions, sweet onions)
- Heat (whole chiles, chile paste, red pepper flakes, hot sauce)
- Fragrant spices (cumin, turmeric, chili powder, smoked paprika, mustard powder)
- Anchovies (YES! And before you say, "No way, anchovies?!" they just add great umami flavor. You will become a believer.)
- Tomato sauce

When All Else Fails, Blend It

I can hear you in my ear right now: "But Mareya, what if I can't stand the texture of a forkful of greens?" Or "If I try kale, I will cry." To that I answer, breathe. Just breathe. Let's transform it. Get your food processor or blender out and break that bad boy down. Throwing them into a smoothie where they get to hang out with fruit, protein, cocoa powder, and chia seeds is the easiest way to get them in without a struggle. You can also mix those blended greens into everything from egg dishes to pizza to soups to sauces. It's a clever way to "hide" them, and practically speaking, you can eat more when they're processed down. For example, when you're making an egg dish, puree a variety of greens like arugula, chard, and watercress and blend them with egg whites to make a "green" omelet and up the antioxidant quotient. You can do the same thing with crepes and even pancakes, adding blended greens to the batter and taking them over to the savory side. Try spinach, shrimp, and feta with romesco sauce over the top. YUUUM!

Whether you're eating them or drinking them, the point is just to get them into your body. A green drink can even be one of your complete meals. Start your day with a Super(s)hero Smoothie (page 99), which I created to encourage my son to get in more greens and other great ingredients, so we wouldn't start the day with tears over texture aversions.

How to Handle Your Greens

Produce starts to decline immediately after being picked, and often our greens are traveling around the world to get to us. One estimate shows that from the time it is picked in the field to when your purchase in the store, it has already lost 45 to 60 percent of its nutrients. When picking cut produce, a green grocer or local farmers' market usually carries food that has traveled less distance. You can now find greens with the roots attached at your grocery store, which helps produce last longer and retains up to 60 percent more of its nutritional value. You can also find herbs and lettuces in their own little hydroponic growing system. This helps you retain as much supercharged nutrient density as possible in every bite. You can literally feel your body buzz from the energy. Growing your own, even if it's in a windowsill herb garden, is a great habit to pick up to feel connected with your food source. Trust me, I have zero backyard but have enough herbage to throw into salads and dishes regularly, and I'm notoriously not a green thumb. If I can do it, you can, too, my friend.

While we often hear about outbreaks of foodborne illness, few of us focus on the number one cause, which is bagged leafy greens. Personally, I think it's nuts to pay double or triple for prewashed greens when you can be more confident about your greens when you wash and store them yourself. Those bloated bags of precut veggies are often swollen because of trapped gas, which means that they have already aged before you take them home.

By thoroughly removing the soils, fertilizers, and handling residue that can harbor bacteria and parasites, you'll retain nutrient density, extend freshness, and get your greens, fruit, and other veggies clean, clean, clean.

When my dad got cancer and was told to avoid raw produce I knew we had to do something to help make our raw fruits and veggies safer. So I invented the eatCleaner line of food wash and wipes to make sure there was a way to get the fresh foods we eat as clean and nutritious as possible. . . . So wash your produce the right way and watch the shift in your energy and overall vibe start rockin'.

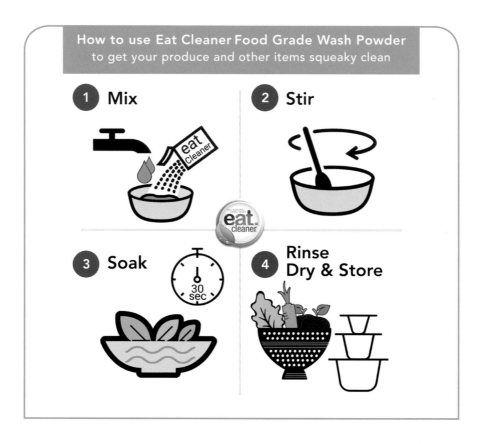

How to use Eat Cleaner Food Grade Wash Powder
to get your produce and other items squeaky clean

1 **Mix**

2 **Stir**

3 **Soak**   30 sec

4 **Rinse Dry & Store**

MAKES 2 SERVINGS

SUPER(S)HERO SMOOTHIE

We could all stand to feel like a super(s)hero, especially in the morning, right? You taste the sweetness of the berries and get the benefit of all the amazing anti-inflammatory ingredients that feed your body and brain—and it tastes *forkin'* great. Double bonus!

½ cup fresh or frozen berries

1 cup baby spinach

2 tablespoons natural almond or peanut butter (or sunflower seed butter, for a nut-free option)

2 cups homemade almond milk (soak 1 cup raw almonds in 5 cups cold water overnight; blend until smooth in a high-powered blender; strain if desired)

2 frozen bananas, peel on and stem and end trimmed (see Note)

2 teaspoons unsweetened cocoa powder

A few drops of liquid stevia

½ cup ice

Combine all the ingredients in a high-speed blender and blend until smooth. Pour into a glass and enjoy!

NOTE: Leaving the peel on the banana means extra nutrients. Just wash them really thoroughly and let them get extra, extra ripe before freezing them or throwing them into the blender.

ROCKIN' RAW SLAW

INGREDIENTS

2 cups shredded red or green cabbage

2 cups shredded Brussels sprouts

1 cup shredded carrots

DRESSING

2 teaspoons raw unfiltered apple cider vinegar

2 tablespoons hemp oil or extra-virgin olive oil

2 tablespoons natural smooth peanut butter (or sunflower seed butter, for a nut-free option)

Juice of 1 lime

2 tablespoons raw honey

Pinch of sea salt

½ teaspoon freshly ground black pepper

1 tablespoon raw hemp hearts

DIRECTIONS

1) In a large bowl, combine the shredded vegetables.

2) MAKE THE DRESSING: Put the vinegar in a medium bowl. While whisking continuously, slowly stream in the hemp oil. Whisk in the peanut butter, lime juice, honey, salt, and pepper until smooth.

3) Pour the dressing over the vegetables and toss to combine. Top with the hemp hearts and serve.

BROCCOLI AND SUN-DRIED TOMATO FRITTATA

INGREDIENTS

Nonstick olive or coconut oil cooking spray

1 teaspoon extra-virgin olive oil

1 medium red onion, finely diced

1 garlic clove, crushed

1 tablespoon finely chopped fresh parsley

2 cups coarsely chopped broccoli

2 tablespoons finely chopped sun-dried tomatoes

½ teaspoon kosher salt

½ teaspoon freshly ground black pepper

3 large eggs

6 large egg whites

3 tablespoons freshly grated Parmesan cheese

DIRECTIONS

1) Preheat the oven to 350°F. Spray a shallow 2-quart baking dish with cooking spray.

2) In a wide nonstick skillet, heat the olive oil over medium heat. Add the onion and cook, stirring often, until it begins to soften, about 3 minutes.

3) Stir in the garlic, parsley, and broccoli. Cook, stirring often, until the broccoli is bright green, about 3 minutes. Add the sun-dried tomatoes and season the mixture with the salt and pepper.

4) In a large bowl, beat the eggs and egg whites until well blended. Stir in the vegetable mixture.

5) Pour the egg-vegetable mixture into the prepared baking dish. Sprinkle evenly with the Parmesan. Bake until the frittata is firm in the center when touched, 25 to 30 minutes. Serve hot or at room temperature.

TOASTED SEAWEED SUSHI STACKS

This is the perfect snack that comes together in no time when you have your rice precooked as part of your #mealprep. Just season it with vinegar and furikake, top it with some fresh avocado, and add a few thin slices of cucumber, microgreens, or radish and an optional dab of wasabi and coconut amino acids to kick up the flavor. They look so gorgeous and appetizing, too, without the cumbersome task of rolling your sushi just right.

INGREDIENTS

2 tablespoons brown rice vinegar

2 teaspoons granulated stevia

1 teaspoon sea salt

1 cup cooked black rice or brown rice

6 large sheets roasted or toasted nori

1 avocado, sliced

2 tablespoons sliced cucumber, radish, or microgreens

1 tablespoon Homemade Furikake Rice Seasoning (recipe follows)

2 teaspoons prepared wasabi (optional)

Coconut amino acids (optional)

DIRECTIONS

1) In a medium bowl, whisk together the vinegar, stevia, and salt. Add the rice, stir gently, and set aside to allow it to fully absorb the vinegar.

2) On a very dry surface, make two stacks of 3 sheets of nori each. Using a knife or a pizza cutter, slice each stack into 8 squares. (Be careful not to get the nori wet, or it won't be pretty.)

3) Top each stack with 1 tablespoon of the vinegar and press it into the nori carefully. Add a few small slices of avocado, sliced cucumber, and a pinch of furikake. Serve topped with wasabi and amino acids, if you want a little kick.

Homemade Furikake Rice Seasoning

I searched high and low for a "clean" furikake, but I couldn't for the life of me find one without nasty fillers. So we're making our own, and it's super easy-peasy. This adds just the right umami touch and flavor to your single-ingredient super grains. Just store this mixture in an airtight spice shaker and it will last for about a month.

INGREDIENTS

¼ cup coarsely chopped toasted nori strips (see Notes)

¼ cup white sesame seeds

¼ cup black sesame seeds

¼ cup loosely packed bonito flakes (fish flakes), usually found in Asian food specialty markets or online

1 teaspoon sea salt

1 teaspoon togarashi seasoning, usually found in Asian food specialty markets or online, or ½ teaspoon ground cayenne pepper

¼ teaspoon granulated stevia

DIRECTIONS

1) In a spice grinder or coffee grinder (see Notes), pulse the nori until ground but still with some flakiness to it (you don't want a powder). Add all the sesame seeds, the bonito flakes, salt, togarashi, and stevia and pulse together until uniform.

2) Store the furikake in an airtight spice container or jar for up to a month. Use it to top your single-ingredient grains, or on veggies or egg bowls.

NOTES: You can find toasted nori strips in the snack section of most natural food stores. If you don't have a spice grinder or coffee grinder, use a food processor or even a mortar and pestle.

CHIMICHURRI SHRIMP AND SHISHITO PEPPER SKEWERS

INGREDIENTS

Nonstick olive or coconut oil cooking spray

2 pounds large (16/20-count) wild-caught shrimp

1 teaspoon grated lime zest

Juice of 1 lime

Pinch of sea salt

Pinch of freshly ground black pepper

1 pound shishito peppers

1½ cups cherry tomatoes

Chimichurri Sauce (page 107)

DIRECTIONS

1) Soak 12 wooden skewers in water for 30 minutes to prevent burning on the grill. Heat a grill to medium-high.

2) In a medium bowl, combine the shrimp, lime zest, lime juice, salt, and black pepper. Set aside to marinate while the grill heats.

3) Drain the skewers and pat dry with a paper towel. Mist them with cooking spray. On each of 4 skewers, thread 4 shrimp. On the remaining skewers, thread the shishito peppers and tomatoes, alternating them. Mist the skewers with cooking spray.

4) Grill the shrimp skewers for 2 minutes on each side, taking care not to burn shrimp. Grill the vegetable skewers until the skins are slightly blistered and charred, 4 to 5 minutes total.

5) Remove the skewers from the grill and brush with Chimichurri Sauce; serve more sauce on the side.

Chimichurri Sauce

INGREDIENTS

1 pasilla or serrano pepper

Nonstick olive or coconut oil cooking spray

2 tablespoons white onion

1 cup fresh cilantro

½ cup fresh parsley

½ cup extra-virgin olive oil

1 tablespoon raw unfiltered apple cider vinegar

2 teaspoons fresh lemon juice

½ teaspoon chipotle chile flakes

DIRECTIONS

1) Preheat the oven to 450°F. Line a baking sheet with parchment paper or a silicone mat.

2) Place the pasilla and serrano peppers on the prepared baking sheet and mist them with cooking spray. Roast until the skins blister, about 20 minutes. Remove from the oven and carefully transfer to a plastic bag; seal and set aside for 10 minutes (this makes the skins easier to remove). Peel the skins from the peppers by rubbing in a plastic bag and remove stems and seeds; transfer the flesh to a food processor.

3) Add the onion, cilantro, parsley, olive oil, vinegar, lemon juice, and chipotle flakes and pulse until smooth.

4) Serve the chimichurri sauce alongside proteins, as a dipping sauce for veggies, or drizzled over eggs. SO good you'll want to eat it with a spoon and slather it on everything.

MOLOKHIA SOUP (SOUP OF THE KINGS)

You may have never seen this herb, the forest green leaves of the jute plant, but we're about to put molokhia (often referred to as Jew's mallow) on the mainstream map. The word *molokhia* means "of the kingdom" in Arabic, because it was a prized food of the pharaohs. They say Cleopatra ate it daily as part of her health and beauty regimen because it's so full of natural collagen, and its rich, verdant color makes it a gorgeous dish. Aside from all these kick-butt benefits, I'm just going to be real: The consistency of this soup is not for everyone. It's a little like okra, but I'm begging you to give it a try. Nutritionally, it has three times the calcium as kale and four times the amount of riboflavin. It also gives you about 70 percent of your RDA for vitamin C and about 25 percent for vitamin A, along with a ton of other minerals and vitamins. It's one of the most nutrient-dense foods on the planet, so it's worth a few goes around the bowl, especially with all the amazing spices in this soup and how it all comes together. My kids were raised on it and so was I.

INGREDIENTS

2 tablespoons ghee (clarified butter)

4 large garlic cloves, minced

½ teaspoon ground cardamom

2 teaspoons ground coriander

1 teaspoon sea salt, plus more as needed

1 (14-ounce) package frozen finely chopped molokhia, found in Middle Eastern food specialty stores or online (do not thaw)

4 cups low-sodium chicken or vegetable broth

Cooked tricolor quinoa or black rice, for serving

DIRECTIONS

1) In a 2-quart or larger saucepan, melt the ghee over medium heat. Add the garlic and cook, stirring, until fragrant, 1 to 2 minutes. Add the cardamom, coriander, and salt and cook for 2 minutes more.

2) Add the frozen molokhia and cook until thawed, 5 to 10 minutes. Add the broth and season with additional salt, if desired. Cook over medium heat for another 10 minutes, until soup has thickened.

3) Serve the molokhia soup over a scoop of tricolor quinoa or black rice with Moroccan Spiced Chicken Legs (page 30) alongside, if desired.

"BURNT" BRUSSELS SPROUTS WITH BLACK GARLIC

INGREDIENTS

2 tablespoons raw coconut oil, melted

6 to 8 fermented black garlic cloves

2 tablespoons tomato paste

1 teaspoon smoked paprika

2 tablespoons balsamic vinegar

Sea salt and freshly ground black pepper

1 pound Brussels sprouts, trimmed and halved through the stem

DIRECTIONS

1) Preheat the oven to 425°F.

2) In a large bowl, whisk together the melted coconut oil, black garlic, tomato paste, paprika, and vinegar and season with salt and pepper. Add the Brussels sprouts and toss to coat.

3) Spread the Brussels sprouts over the prepared pan in an even layer and roast for 20 to 25 minutes, until well browned and tender. Roast for a few extra minutes if you like the consistency a little more "burnt."

VEGGIE CABBAGE FRIED "RICE"

INGREDIENTS

2 tablespoons raw coconut oil

2 teaspoons toasted sesame oil

3 garlic cloves, minced

1 head green cabbage, processed in food processor until ricelike

1 bunch Tuscan (lacinato or dinosaur) kale, finely chopped

3 large eggs

2 tablespoons coconut amino acids

½ teaspoon ground ginger

½ teaspoon red chile paste

4 scallions, chopped

1 tablespoon black sesame seeds

Chopped peanuts, for garnish

DIRECTIONS

1) In a wok or large skillet, heat the coconut oil and sesame oil over medium heat. Add the garlic and cook, stirring, until translucent. Add the cabbage and kale and sauté for about 3 minutes.

2) In a bowl, whisk together the eggs, coconut aminos, ginger, and red chile paste. Add the egg mixture to the wok and stir until well incorporated. Cook for 2 minutes, then remove from the heat and toss in the scallions and sesame seeds. Top with a sprinkle of chopped peanuts and serve.

ASIAN-SPICED PULLED PORK AND GREENS BOWL

The fragrance of this slow-cooked pork is so insanely good, it's going to waft into your neighbor's home, so don't be surprised if you eat this with unexpected guests. Oh, wait, you didn't want that? Make sure to leave a bowl on your doorstep as a goodwill offering. When you add the greens, quickled veggies, and black rice, it doesn't get any better. This is the perfect meal-prep dish, and a feast for the eyes. . . . Love manifested in a bowl.

PULLED PORK

1 cup low-sodium chicken broth

½ cup red cooking wine

¼ cup coconut amino acids

1 teaspoon grated orange zest

Juice of 1 large orange

3 star anise pods

3 garlic cloves, minced

1 tablespoon Chinese five-spice powder

2 teaspoons sea salt

1 teaspoon ground white pepper

3 pounds boneless pork shoulder

BOWLS

3 cups cooked black rice

2 tablespoons Homemade Furikake Rice Seasoning (page 104)

Rainbow Veggie Quickles (page 76)

Collard greens, sautéed

DIRECTIONS

1) MAKE THE PULLED PORK: In a medium bowl, whisk together all the ingredients except for the pork.

2) Put the pork shoulder in a large slow cooker and pour the broth mixture over the top, making sure it's drenched. Cover and cook on high for 5 hours or low for 8 hours, until the pork is fork-tender.

3) Remove the pork from the cooking liquid and shred the meat using two forks. Return the pulled pork to the liquid in the slow cooker and toss thoroughly. If desired, cover and cook on high for 30 minutes to allow the shredded pork to absorb more flavor.

4) ASSEMBLE THE BOWLS: In each bowl, layer the pulled pork, ½ cup cooked black rice, 1 teaspoon furikake, quickles, and sautéed collard greens.

CURRY CASHEW CHICKEN LETTUCE CUPS

INGREDIENTS

1 pound chicken breasts, poached and cubed

½ cup diced celery

½ cup diced cored Fuji, Gala, or Pink Lady apple

¼ cup cashew pieces, toasted

¼ cup currants

DRESSING

1 cup plain Greek yogurt

1½ tablespoons Dijon mustard

1 tablespoon fresh lemon juice

2 teaspoons curry powder

1 teaspoon each sea salt and ground white pepper, plus more as needed

½ teaspoon ground ginger

12 whole butter lettuce leaves, for serving

1 tablespoon raw hemp hearts (optional)

DIRECTIONS

1) In a large bowl toss together the chicken, celery, apple, cashews, and currants.

2) MAKE THE DRESSING: In a small bowl, whisk together all the dressing ingredients until smooth.

3) Pour the dressing over the chicken mixture and toss until well coated. Adjust the seasoning as needed.

4) Serve scoops of the chicken salad in the butter lettuce leaves and top with a sprinkle of hemp hearts, if desired, for an added omega-3 boost and a nice little pop of texture.

THE FAST
BREAK

Do you ever feel like some days your appetite is "healthier"—meaning you're so famished, you could eat a yoga mat—while other days, you can breeze by on a smoothie? Of course, if you've worked out like a fiend, you can attribute your hunger to an expenditure of calories. Otherwise, it's probably your hormones. Leptin (which suppresses appetite) and ghrelin (which makes you feel hungrier) can get thrown out of balance, along with metabolic hormones like insulin, cortisol (a stress hormone), and estrogen. If you're sleep-deprived and stretched in a hundred different directions, I don't have to tell you how many snack-size chocolates and bags of chips will pay the price. Your body is in a constant state of trying to balance different hormones that speak different languages, and your brain, the interpreter, is usually at a rave.

Imagine cortisol, your stress hormone, trying to talk leptin, your hunger-reducing hormone, out of eating a pint of ice cream while you're standing in front of the freezer. It's easy to see how a major communication breakdown would ensue, as they have different agendas and will battle it out with spoons until they get what they want. Your job is to raise the white flag—and give your poor body a break, while getting all your troops marching together. Your relationships, mood, and energy will get down on their knees to thank you.

This part of *Eat Like You Give a Fork* explores intermittent fasting, meaning we are going to restrict the time frame of when the kitchen—and your mouth—is open for business. I call this the Fast Break. Just like in basketball, you take the offense and steam ahead toward the basket quickly, so the defense never has a chance to think. We're going for all net from the free-throw line, baby!

Intermittent fasting has become popular, and for good reason. Not only does it help give you a chance to realign and restore, but it can also be incredibly effective in optimizing fat burning, disease prevention, and a ton of other awesome benefits. Intermittent fasting has been associated with:

- **Accelerated weight loss**

- **Extended life span**

- **Improved cardiovascular health**

- **Decreased cancer risk**

- **Prevention of chronic degenerative diseases**

- **Improved mood**

- **Reduced digestive stress**

- **Improved sleep**

I don't know about you, but I think most people could all use a lot of that!

Fast Break to Fat-Burning Success

If you've ever gotten into a rut with your workouts where you stopped seeing results, you were probably advised to "mix up" your routine to avoid hitting an exercise plateau. Varying your eating patterns works in the same way, so to fast-track success, we'll use food cycling a couple of times a week to mix up your habits, allowing you to reset and rev up what I call your fat-burning intelligence quotient (FBIQ). Your body is smart and knows how to do this naturally. You just have to shift it into gear. In my personal experience, intermittent fasting with a focus on plant-based eating has been one of the most powerful fat-loss methods I've implemented.

> Food cycling allows you to reset and rev up your fat-burning intelligence quotient (FBIQ).

For our approach to food cycling, we're going to do a form of food elimination with compressed eating windows for two days each week, Tuesday and Thursday. This is an intermittent vegan fast. You won't be eating any animal products on these days, and you will compress your meals into an eight-hour window. Before you think, *Fork you, sister, you're going to starve me to death!* I promise this isn't about eating soy substitutes for every animal protein, which leaves you lamenting the lackluster imposter or feeling so hungry you want to gnaw on your chopsticks. We are simply giving you a chance to reboot by giving your digestion a break. And the good news is, if you do this regularly, your body will embrace the shift and get into a hot little rhythm.

Eight Life-Changing Reasons for Going Vegan Two Days per Week

1. Research conducted at the Harvard School of Public Health has found that eating even small amounts of red meat, especially processed red meat, on a regular basis is linked to an increased risk of heart disease and stroke.

2. Eating purely plant foods requires mindfulness and intentionality, tuning in to what you are preparing and eating. When you connect with what is on that fork, you become acutely aware of what you are putting in your piehole (I mean this with love).

3. An intentional reset favoring fruits, vegetables, nuts, seeds, soy, plant-based fat, and single-ingredient grains two days per week breaks the grip animal products have on your taste buds and your health

4. Vegan eating gives your body a rest from the overtime your organs have put in to metabolize meat. The focus on hydrating fruits and vegetables helps your body release toxins and provides a flood of much-needed nutrients.

5. Eating more vegetables adds bulk and fiber to your diet. Vegetables aid digestion and move things along. You're building a stronger gut, digestion, and ability to eliminate well. I don't have to tell you how important it is to keep the pipes clean, if you know what I mean.

6. Vegan fasting also bolsters our self-discipline since it eliminates certain options and focuses us on what we can select. It will help you hone your ability to make good food choices across the board.

7. Engaging in vegan fasting on the same two days per week sets up a rhythm in both your meal planning and food preparation, so your commitment becomes easy, expected, and welcomed. It will quickly become the natural way you eat, rather than feeling like you're making an effort.

8. Have you ever felt your body vibrate from all the plant-based love it's getting? It will, quite literally, help you feel grounded. Don't be surprised if you experience more restful sleep, a better frame of mind, and the urge to hug everyone around you.

I grew up in the Coptic Orthodox tradition, in which intermittent vegan fasting is a mainstay. We believe a spiritual connection forms during vegan fasting that deeply connects us with both our humanity and divinity. I always say the higher the plant, the closer to God. Even if you aren't spiritual in that sense, intermittently eating vegan puts you in touch with the earth and the life force that food can be.

I took a group to Italy to do a weeklong immersion in farm-to-table Italian cooking. We stayed in a brick-and-terra-cotta villa nestled in a grove of over three hundred silvery-leafed olive trees in the hills above Pisa. A sign hung in the dining room that read, *We give thanks to the fruits of the air, of the earth, above and below its surface, to the animals and to the elements, alchemic nourishment for our body and our essence. May our behavior be conscious and dignified.* While we prepared our evening meals, we nibbled on cubes of pecorino cheese and giant green olives harvested from the trees on the property, then sat to enjoy the experience with every ounce of presence. It fed our souls and nourished our spirits.

I was explaining the concept to my yoga instructor, and he said, "That's called the yogi meal." You eat with intention because you've selected those foods. You savor every bite slowly. You enjoy the meal with family and friends. You really taste each morsel, the individual ingredients, the spices, and the love and reverence that made the dish.

Forming a new habit is what we're after, and experts say this takes about twenty-one days. We're going to start now. Take out your smartphone and set a calendar reminder for yourself. Every Tuesday and Thursday, you're going to note what time you consume your first meal and finish your last meal within eight hours of that time. Your window could be breakfast at 10 a.m. and finishing dinner by 6 p.m. This will allow you to eat at a time that's not too late in the evening, but late enough that your stomach isn't growling in the middle of the night. Remember to think of this as a break for your system versus a time of deprivation. You won't feel the need to feed on meat and dairy on these days when you combine your plant-based proteins and fats for optimal EAAs. Follow the recipes here for new and fun hearty vegan meals that'll fill you up.

GET MIGHTY WITH THE GREEN LEAF

Tea is a tradition in many countries, and for good reason. Looking at the research, one might think this little green leaf could save the world. Green tea, including the super-antioxidant powerhouse matcha tea, which is ground whole tea leaves, is linked to fighting cancer and heart disease, lowering cholesterol, burning fat, preventing diabetes and stroke, and staving off dementia, just to name a few benefits. Green tea contains a variety of enzymes, amino acids, carbohydrates, lipids, sterols, polyphenols, carotenoids, tocopherols, vitamins, caffeine and related compounds, phytochemicals, and dietary minerals that are great for your body.

Create an afternoon tea tradition as a time to take a breather from your desk, your bills, gas prices, social media chain messages, or whatever raises your blood pressure.

- Strive to drink half your body weight in ounces of water (this includes unsweetened tea or fresh vegetable juice)—not the sugar-laden, made-from-concentrate stuff—every day. Example: If you weigh 200 pounds, drink 100 ounces of water per day, which is about twelve 8-ounce cups.

- Keep an insulated water bottle near you at all times to encourage regular guzzling of cold/warm liquids. Ideally, find a bottle that's an easy portion of what you need daily. For example, if you're after about 72 ounces a day, get a 36-ounce bottle and fill it twice—once before noon and once before you go to bed . . . but not too late, so you don't disrupt your sacred sleep
- Drink warm beverages with food and cold beverages between meals.

Between the Bites

Outside your eight-hour eating window, I want you to grow a hump like you're a camel. Hydration is equally or even more essential to your success as your new habits and food wardrobe are. You can live without food for weeks, but without water, your system will shut down within a few days. Even though setting that 64-ounce soda or 20-ounce latte to the side seems like the end of your existence, you can live without them, and you won't miss them after you start asking, "What have you done for me lately, latte?" Just recognize how important pure, natural spring water is to maintaining a healthy weight and vibrancy.

- The human body as a whole is more than 60 percent water.

- Blood is 92 percent water.

- The brain and muscles are 75 percent water.

- Bones are about 22 percent water.

Every metabolic function your cells perform requires hydration. It's that important! In fact, being dehydrated can fool you into the sensation of feeling hungry. Keep your system from getting clogged up. With lots of pure water, you'll have fewer cravings. Having a bottle of water and a mug nearby will help reinforce the habit of consistent hydration.

Here's an important note that most people don't realize. Drinking ice-cold bevvies with food slows down digestion and can cause fats to stop up your system. So if you're slurping down an iced tea and thinking it's better than an ice-cold soda, you're only part right. Drink warm water, warm tea, or Real Vitality Tonic (page 47) with food to encourage digestion. Between meals, down those icy drinks to speed up metabolism. Flavor water naturally with some sliced cucumber, mint, or some lemon and lime wedges. Get a little tropical and add fresh strawberries, pineapple, or any seasonal fruit you have on hand. Fill an ice cube tray with slices of fresh fruit, citrus, or cucumber wedges, and freeze to add color and flavor to your glass without any added sugar, chemicals, or other garbage.

NEW JACKFRUIT CITY

Looking at a jackfruit, you'd probably think, *How could this giant spiky dinosaur-egg-looking thing be a fruit?* In fact, it's the king of fruit—the largest tree fruit around—and a low-calorie source of fiber. It's gotten really popular as a vegan meat replacement because its brownish flesh is so meaty-looking; it's a fresh ringer for shredded chicken, carnitas, or ground taco meat, depending on how it's used. It is a massively large fruit that's hard to peel and break down without a really, really big knife. Luckily, they've done the work for us, and packages of precut jackfruit are readily available. You don't know jackfruit if you haven't tried it.

PUREED VEGGIE LENTIL SOUP

Growing up, this was one of my favorite dishes ever. I love the consistency of the lentils when they're pureed with all the veggies, which gives the dish great depth. And just the right amount of heat from the cayenne hits the spot! You may even be able to get the texture-averse in your tribe on board with this version.

INGREDIENTS

2 tablespoons olive oil

1 cup finely chopped red onion

½ cup finely chopped carrot

½ cup finely chopped celery

1 teaspoon sea salt or kosher salt

16 ounces uncooked lentils, rinsed

1 teaspoon freshly ground black pepper

1 teaspoon ground coriander

½ teaspoon cayenne pepper

2 quarts low-sodium vegetable broth

Optional but recommended: Dukkah seasoning to top soup

DIRECTIONS

1) In a large stockpot, heat the olive oil over medium heat. Add the onion, carrot, celery, and salt and sweat until the onion is translucent, 6 to 7 minutes.

2) Add the lentils and cook, stirring, for 2 minutes. Add the black pepper, coriander, and cayenne and stir to combine. Add the broth and increase the heat to high. Bring the mixture just to a boil, then reduce the heat to low, cover, and cook at a low simmer until the lentils are tender, 45 to 55 minutes.

3) Using an immersion blender, puree the soup directly in the pot until mostly smooth, but with a little texture left. (You can also transfer the soup to a regular blender in batches, taking care not to burn yourself with the hot liquid.)

4) Ladle your soup into a bowl and top with a pinch of dukkah.

THAI COCONUT PUMPKIN SOUP

INGREDIENTS

1½ teaspoons raw coconut oil or grapeseed oil

2 tablespoons finely diced red onion

1 garlic clove, crushed

1 small red chile, seeded and finely chopped (be careful of the seeds and your eyes), or ½ teaspoon red pepper flakes

2 tablespoons yellow curry paste

3 cups low-sodium vegetable broth

Two (15-ounce) cans pure pumpkin puree

1 teaspoon sea salt

1 (13.5-ounce) can light coconut milk

1 tablespoon chopped fresh cilantro (optional)

DIRECTIONS

1) In a large saucepan, melt the coconut oil over medium-low heat. Add the onion and garlic and cook until translucent, taking care not to brown them. Add the chile and stir.

2) Add the curry paste and sauté until fragrant, about 3 minutes. Add the broth and the pumpkin and whisk until well incorporated and creamy; season with sea salt.

3) Add the coconut milk and cook for a few minutes.

4) Remove from the heat and garnish with the cilantro, if desired.

BALSAMIC ROASTED VEGGIES WITH TOASTED TURMERIC CHIA SEEDS

INGREDIENTS

2 tablespoons Dijon mustard

¼ cup balsamic vinegar

2 tablespoons raw coconut oil, melted

2 tablespoons coconut amino acids

1 teaspoon ground white pepper

1 medium head cauliflower, cut into bite-size florets

1 medium head broccoli, cut into bite-size florets

2 cups halved Brussels sprouts

2 teaspoons ground turmeric

1 teaspoon chia seeds

DIRECTIONS

1) Preheat the oven to 375°F.

2) In a large bowl, whisk together the mustard, vinegar, coconut oil, amino acids, and white pepper. Add the vegetables and toss to coat with the dressing. Spread the vegetables evenly over a baking sheet.

3) In a small dry skillet, toast the turmeric and chia seeds over low heat for 2 minutes, taking care not to burn them. Remove from the heat and sprinkle the spices over the vegetables.

4) Bake for 30 minutes, or until the vegetables are golden brown. Enjoy!

BROCCOLINI ALL'ARRABBIATA

Arrabbiata means "angry" in Italian, but there's no way you're feeling hangry or angry after eating what I call the magic broccoli. It's just that good. If you can't find broccolini, just use regular broccoli, including the stalks. That's the most nutrient-dense part of the plant! Peel the tough skin and slice them all the way down into 1-inch spears. I include hemp hearts in this spicy little dish for some more good fat and a little added pop.

INGREDIENTS

Sea salt

1½ to 2 pounds broccolini

4 tablespoons extra-virgin olive oil

1 lemon, cut in half

½ medium yellow onion, finely chopped

2 garlic cloves, minced

1 teaspoon red pepper flakes

1 (28-ounce) can no-salt-added crushed San Marzano tomatoes (see Note)

1 teaspoon Himalayan pink salt

½ teaspoon ground white pepper

2 tablespoons raw hemp hearts

DIRECTIONS

1) Bring 6 cups salted water to a boil in a large pot. Fill a large bowl with ice and water. Add the broccolini to the boiling water and cook for 1 minute. Transfer the broccolini to the ice water to stop the cooking process. Drain and set aside.

2) In a large skillet, heat 2 tablespoons of the olive oil over medium heat. Add blanched broccolini and sauté for 3 minutes, taking care not to overcook it. Transfer the broccolini to a serving plate. Add the lemon halves to the hot pan, cut-side down, and sear for 20 to 30 seconds. Squeeze the lemon juice over the broccolini.

3) In the same skillet, heat the remaining 2 tablespoons olive oil over medium heat. Add the onion and cook, stirring until translucent, 7 to 8 minutes. Add the garlic and red pepper flakes and sauté for another minute.

4) Add the tomatoes, pink salt, and white pepper and reduce the heat to low. Cook until the mixture has reduced by half, about 20 minutes. Remove from the heat and add the hemp hearts.

5) Spoon the sauce over the broccolini and serve. (Save any extra sauce for squash noodles or your Saucy Italian Stuffed Mushrooms, page 190.)

NOTE: Use canned regular whole peeled tomatoes if you can't find San Marzanos, but they're worth the search.

FUL MUDAMMAS (STEWED BROWN FAVA BEANS)

When I was a baby, I had a hard time nursing or keeping down the expensive formula my parents had to hunt through Egypt to find. In desperation, they turned to fava beans, commonly known as ful, the national staple of Egypt's poor and rich and everyone in between. I know what you're thinking: You were raised on bean juice? Didn't that make you really gassy? The gravy that's made when you stew fava beans for twelve hours is so rich in protein and amino acids that it became my sustenance. My parents would go to the corner fava bean cart—the food trucks back then—and Amm Soona, the jovial, bald proprietor who felt sorry for my parents, would reserve bags of the velvety brown liquid for me to suck down by the bottle. I'm proud to say I am "powered by bean juice."

INGREDIENTS

2 cups cooked or canned brown fava beans (drained, liquid reserved, and rinsed if canned; see Note) found at Middle East specialty food markets or online

2 teaspoons ground cumin

1 teaspoon ground coriander

1 teaspoon garlic powder

2 teaspoons extra-virgin olive oil, plus more for drizzling

Himalayan pink salt and freshly ground black pepper

OPTIONAL TOPPINGS

Tahini (up to 2 teaspoons per serving)

Hard-boiled egg (up to 1 egg per serving)

Fresh arugula

Tomatoes

Pickled red onions

DIRECTIONS

1) In a medium saucepan, combine the fava beans, 1 cup water (or the reserved liquid from the can), the cumin, coriander, and garlic powder. Cook over medium heat until the mixture begins to bubble, then reduce the heat to medium-low and cook for 10 minutes more, until much of the liquid has been absorbed.

2) Remove from the heat and add olive oil. Mash the beans with the back of a fork.

3) Serve in bowls, topped with a drizzle of extra-virgin olive oil and the optional toppings of your choice.

NOTE: Substitute pinto beans if you can't find fava beans. But do yourself a fava' and find favas!

BAKED SESAME SEED FALAFEL PATTIES WITH LEMONY TAHINI SAUCE

I know it might seem like a little bit of a pain to use dried chickpeas, but trust me. These baked falafel patties will take on an amazing texture if you do it this way versus using canned chickpeas. If all else fails, go canned—they'll still be amazing—and go for the sesame seed coating. That's the authentic Egyptian way, and it adds a great boost of MUFAs—monounsaturated fatty acids that help to lower cholesterol and keep your ticker tip top! Serve these with add-ons like onion and turnip quickles (page 76). You can also wrap them in butter lettuce leaves for fala-fully good wraps.

INGREDIENTS

1¾ cups dried chickpeas, picked over

2 garlic cloves

1 small yellow onion, quartered

1 tablespoon ground cumin

1 teaspoon cayenne pepper

1 cup fresh cilantro or parsley, coarsely chopped

1½ teaspoons sea salt

½ teaspoon freshly ground black pepper

½ teaspoon baking soda

1 tablespoon fresh lemon juice

¼ cup white sesame seeds

Nonstick olive or coconut oil cooking spray

½ cup Lemony Tahini Sauce (recipe follows), for serving

DIRECTIONS

1) Put the chickpeas in a large bowl and add water to cover by 3 or 4 inches. Soak for 24 hours, adding more water as needed so they stay covered. After soaking, you should be able to break them apart between your fingers.

2) Preheat the oven to 375°F. Line a baking sheet with parchment paper or a silicone baking mat.

3) Drain the chickpeas and transfer them to a food processor. Add the garlic, onion, cumin, cayenne, cilantro, 1 teaspoon of the salt, pepper, baking soda, and lemon juice. Pulse until everything is minced but not pureed, stopping the machine and scraping down the sides if necessary; add water 1 tablespoon at a time, if necessary, to allow the machine to do its work, but keep the mixture as dry as possible. Taste and adjust the seasoning, adding more salt, pepper, or cayenne as needed.

4) Using an ice cream scoop, portion the mixture into 20 balls, 1½ to 2 inches each, then flatten into thick patties. Pour the sesame seeds over a plate. Press the patties into the sesame seeds to coat both sides and place them on the prepared baking sheet. Mist them on both sides with cooking spray. Bake until golden all over, 10 to 12 minutes on each side.

5) Serve the baked falafel hot or at room temperature, drizzled with the tahini sauce.

Lemony Tahini Sauce

MAKES 4 SERVINGS

INGREDIENTS

½ cup tahini (sesame paste)

2 garlic cloves, crushed

Juice of 1 lemon

1 tablespoon raw unfiltered apple cider vinegar

1 tablespoon extra-virgin olive oil, plus more if desired

¼ teaspoon Himalayan pink salt

1 tablespoon minced fresh parsley

¼ teaspoon paprika

DIRECTIONS

1) In a small bowl, stir together the tahini and ¼ cup lukewarm water until smooth.

2) Stir in the garlic, lemon juice, vinegar, and olive oil. Season with salt.

3) Top with fresh parsley and paprika and serve with olive oil drizzled on top, if desired (in Egyptian culture, this is kind of mandatory).

THE ULTIMATE FROZEN BUDDHA BOWL

INGREDIENTS

½ frozen banana, peel left on

One 3.5 oz. packet frozen no-sugar-added açaí or pitaya

1 teaspoon ground flaxseed

¼ cup unsweetened nondairy milk (almond, rice, coconut, soy, hemp)

½ teaspoon raw coconut oil

1 cup plain coconut yogurt

½ teaspoon spirulina powder

½ teaspoon raw honey

OPTIONAL TOPPINGS

Pomegranate arils

Fresh pataya and lychee fruit

Grape halves

Hulled sunflower seeds or raw hemp hearts

Maca powder

Unsweetened cocoa powder

DIRECTIONS

1) In a food processor or blender, combine the banana, açaí, flaxseed, milk, and coconut oil. Blend on medium to high speed for 15 to 30 seconds, until smooth and creamy. Pour into a bowl and add the yogurt, spirulina, and honey. Stir until completely smooth.

2) Top your Buddha bowl with an assortment of topping and feel zenlike immediately. Serve it in a fresh pitaya bowl to be super extra.

BROILED TEMPEH STRIPS WITH HEMP-PINEAPPLE SALSA

Hemp is a product of the cannabis sativa plant, but these seeds won't make you fly. They will, however, contribute incredible benefits, delivering essential-fatty-acid-quality plant protein and minerals. . . . And it's great for your skin. Hemp offers such balanced nutrition, you could survive on it. Chew on that!

HEMP-PINEAPPLE SALSA

1 teaspoon lime zest

Juice of 1 lime

1 tablespoon hemp oil or hemp seeds, ground

½ teaspoon freshly ground black pepper

½ teaspoon ground turmeric

¼ teaspoon smoked sea salt

1 tablespoon raw honey

1 cup shredded red or green cabbage

1 cup chopped fresh pineapple

3 tablespoons chopped fresh cilantro

1 jalapeño or serrano pepper, finely minced

¼ large red onion

1 pound organic tempeh, cut into 1-inch strips

2 tablespoons toasted sesame oil

DIRECTIONS

1) Preheat the oven to broil.

2) MAKE THE SALSA: In a small bowl, whisk together the lime zest, lime juice, hemp oil, pepper, turmeric, salt, and honey.

3) In a medium bowl, combine the cabbage, pineapple, cilantro, jalapeño, and onion. Add lime juice dressing and toss to combine.

4) Put the tempeh on a baking sheet and brush with the sesame oil. Broil until the texture is firm and the tempeh turns golden brown, about 10 minutes.

5) Top the tempeh with the salsa and serve.

SMOKY VEGGIE, JACKFRUIT, AND WHITE BEAN CHILI

INGREDIENTS

1½ teaspoons raw coconut oil

½ cup chopped onion

8 ounces jackfruit, shredded (see Note)

2 chipotle chiles in adobo sauce, plus 1 teaspoon adobo sauce from the can (these are spicy)

½ cup chopped bell pepper

2 zucchini, chopped

1 clove fresh garlic, minced

2 teaspoons ground cumin

1 teaspoon dried oregano

1 teaspoon smoked paprika

1 (14-ounce) can low-sodium or no-salt-added crushed tomatoes

1 cup low-sodium vegetable broth

1¾ cups cooked cannellini or great northern beans, or 1 (15-ounce) can, drained and rinsed

2 tablespoons tomato paste

Sliced avocado (optional)

DIRECTIONS

1) In a large stockpot, melt the coconut oil over medium-high heat.

2) Add the onion and sauté for 3 minutes.

3) Add the jackfruit and sauté for 3 minutes. Add chipotles, adobo sauce, and bell pepper and sauté for 2 minutes more.

4) Add the garlic, cumin, oregano, and paprika and cook for 1 minute. Add the tomatoes and broth and bring to a boil. Reduce the heat to low, cover, and simmer for 15 minutes.

5) Stir in the beans and tomato paste and bring back to a boil. Reduce the heat to low and simmer for 20 to 25 minutes, until the mixture has thickened and the liquid has reduced.

6) Serve hot, topped with crispy sprouted tortilla strips and slices of fresh avocado, if desired.

NOTE: You can find peeled jackfruit in the refrigerated section.

CINNAMON AND VANILLA DATE SHAKE

The creamiest, dreamiest shake on planet Earth. If you close your eyes, you might mistake it for an ice cream shake, but it's totally dairy-free.

INGREDIENTS

1 cup almonds

½ frozen banana, peel left on

6 pitted dates

1 teaspoon ground cinnamon

½ teaspoon pure vanilla extract

½ cup ice

A few drops liquid stevia, or 1 teaspoon granulated stevia

DIRECTIONS

1) Put the almonds in a storage container, add enough water to cover, cover the container, and soak overnight. Drain and rinse.

2) In a high-speed blender, combine the soaked almonds with 2 cups water and pulse until smooth. Strain, if needed (if you pulse enough, it should not need straining because a little texture is nice), and return the almond milk to the blender. Add the banana and pulse until smooth. Add the dates, cinnamon, vanilla, stevia, and ice and blend until creamy and smooth.

3) Serve immediately with a straw. Enjoy!

APPLE PIE PROTEIN FIT BITES

These are my solution for your sweet tooth, forgoing those expensive bars that are often FWC (filled with crap). They're so nutrient-dense, you can have them for breakfast or as a pre-/post-workout snack. Pie for breakfast? Don't mind if I do!

INGREDIENTS

1½ cups quick-cooking oats

2 tablespoons low-sugar plant-based protein powder

2 teaspoons granulated stevia, or 10–12 drops liquid stevia

1 teaspoon ground cinnamon

¼ teaspoon ground nutmeg

¼ Fuji or Honeycrisp apple, cored and finely diced

¼ cup slivered almonds

TOPPING

2 tablespoons granulated stevia

½ teaspoon ground cinnamon

DIRECTIONS

1) In a medium bowl, combine the oats, protein powder, stevia, cinnamon, and nutmeg. Add hot water 1 tablespoon at a time, until a doughlike consistency is reached and the mixture can be formed into a ball. (If you add too much water at once, you'll have oatmeal. If that happens, just add more oats.) Let cool slightly. Add the apples and almonds and incorporate evenly into the dough.

2) Freeze the mixture for about 15 minutes.

3) Combine all the topping ingredients in a bowl. Roll the oat mixture into 1-inch balls and then roll each in the topping until evenly coated. Freeze in an airtight container for grab-and-go snacks, clean desserts, and pre-/post-workout energy boosts.

CREAMY DREAMY COCOA PUDDING

If you've read the ingredients and wondered how pudding will manifest from chickpeas as the first ingredient, you're gonna have to trust me. I promise it comes together and tastes like a pillowy cloud from heaven.

INGREDIENTS

1 (15-ounce) can chickpeas, drained and rinsed

¾ cup unsweetened cocoa powder

¼ cup cashews

5 dates, pitted

¼ cup unsweetened homemade almond milk plus more to taste

2 teaspoons granulated stevia or 10–12 drops liquid stevia

½ teaspoon pure vanilla extract

OPTIONAL

Coconut whip topping and fruit

DIRECTIONS

1) In a food processor, combine the chickpeas, cocoa powder, cashews, and dates and pulse until smooth.

2) In a small bowl, whisk together the almond milk, stevia, and vanilla. Add the mixture to the food processor with the chickpea mixture and pulse until thick and creamy; add more if you like a thinner consistency.

3) Serve with assorted fruits, including sliced apples, strawberries, banana, and blueberries and coconut whip topping, if desired.

TART CHERRY COCONUT SORBET

This recipe is just too easy and simple to be true. Five ingredients come together like magic, and voilà—dessert is ready. Tart cherries are high in antioxidants and are great for lowering inflammation so they're a natural pain reliever. A bowl of tart cherry coconut sorbet keeps the doctor away!

INGREDIENTS

1½ cups fresh or frozen pitted tart cherries plus ½ cup for topping

4 cups unsweetened coconut yogurt

1½ teaspoons pure vanilla extract

½ cup raw honey

¼ cup blanched sliced almonds

DIRECTIONS

1) Set aside ½ cup of the cherries and put the remaining 1 cup in a food processor. Add the remaining ingredients and pulse until smooth.

2) Pour the mixture into a freezer-safe glass or plastic container, cover, and freeze for about 1 hour. Remove the sorbet from the freezer and run an ice cream scoop over the surface, scraping and stirring it up to remove any iciness. Top the mixture with the reserved ½ cup cherries and blanched almonds and return it to the freezer for at least 3 to 4 hours.

3) Scoop into bowls and savor each spoon.

NOTE: This may melt kind of quickly so keep well frozen in between scoops.

GO GLUTEN-FREE SUPER GRAINS

Carbs have gotten a bad rap, and the idea that you have to avoid them—or worse, eliminate them entirely—is pretty much BS.

Did I just hear your fork drop?

We've heard a lot about carbs being the foundation of the evil empire, as if the mere utterance of the word is enough to make you gain five pounds and become permanently bloated. The confusion lies in the fact that carbohydrates show up in myriad forms. Carbs are also an integral component of fruit, vegetables, grains, nuts, seeds, legumes, milk, and milk products. They have a really important place in your diet and can deliver a ton of nutrients, including amino acids, especially if you're vegan or vegetarian.

Avoiding the whole grain category and saying they don't have a place in your life is like avoiding exercise because you might pull a muscle. The benefits of squats far outweigh the risk; it's just a matter of proportion and proper form. The same goes for grains. When evaluating whether to bite, the question should really be: Which foods will crank my blood sugar? Carbs with high starch content—typically white bread, refined flours, sweets, and processed snacks—are the problem.

> Carbs have a really important place in your diet, and can deliver a ton of nutrients, including amino acids.

Grains that are "clean carbs," often referred to as slow-burning carbs, won't spike your blood sugar, are largely unprocessed and nutrient-dense, and play such an important role on your Give a Fork plan. If you're gluten-intolerant, this is happy dance news, because all the choices here are on your fly list.

I want to help you undo all the preconceived notions you might have. Off to nutrition therapy class we go!

Let's boil it down: There's a huge difference between processed whole flour products (baked goods like muffins, bread, desserts, cookies, and snack foods) and single ingredient, gluten-free super grains (Cue Beyoncé, "*All the single grainies, all the single grainies . . .*"). The "super" kind usually fall in the ancient grains category, and when they're in their whole state, they're loaded with B vitamins, magnesium, protein (that's right!), and nutrients that aid in fat burning. Plus, they're a high source of fiber, which can lower your risk for heart disease and high cholesterol and heal your gut.

How do you distinguish the good, the bad, and the fugly (forkin' ugly)? It comes down to this—how can they benefit your body? Here's a brief survey to help evaluate if that grain is worth your saliva:

1. **Is it minimally processed?**
2. **Is it in its whole form?**
3. **Is it without any added ingredients that you don't recognize?**
4. **Is it grown on a plant (versus manufactured in a plant)?**
5. **Does it taste good?**
6. **Does it contain detectable nutrients?**

If the answer to all of these is yes, your carb selection may very well be a candidate for consumption and thorough, guilt-free enjoyment.

Carbohydrates, specifically grains, can do the following:

- Help feed your brain with glucose. Seriously, your cells and organs need it!
- Offer a great source of fiber to keep you regular. Keeping toxins moving is so important to your overall health. And no one likes to feel clogged up.
- Make you feel good by encouraging the production of serotonin. The more feel-good juice coursing through your veins, the better!
- Give you a quick boost of energy. This helps keep you from crashing through the afternoon and is great for a pre-workout pick-me-up.
- Load you up with stress-reducing vitamins. These can help you manage stuff without freaking out, ya know?
- Feed you to the core with minerals that boost metabolism and stoke the fire to burn, burn, burn fat.

Size Does Matter

Grains add texture and can help you feel fuller and more satisfied for longer. Usually the problem is in the portion sizes. That massive serving of pasta you get at most restaurants isn't a portion, it's a trough! When you Eat Like You Give a Fork, you don't have to be scared of carbing out. About 25 percent of your daily intake of nutrients can be dedicated to a variety of gluten-free super grains, breakfast to dinner and snacks in between, and still turn your body into a fat-burning monster machine.

But enough about the science. What about the flavor? Putting your fork into a bowl of perfectly cooked farro risotto studded with pan-roasted multicolored cauliflower and topped with a little shaving of fresh pecorino cheese is the equivalent of carnal pleasure. Don't deprive yourself of something that contributes to your vibrant health and knows how to satisfy you in more ways than one. The key is to bring out the grains' best texture so they don't dry up on you.

An electric rice cooker is one of the best ways to cook whole grains like quinoa, wheat berries, and others to perfection (we'll bite into those other grains in a bit). The best part is, you don't need to supervise the process. You can infuse flavor into the cooking liquid, and the toppings are a way to kick things up a notch. Waking up to a bowl of warm buckwheat steeped in coconut milk topped with unsweetened shredded coconut, chopped almonds, and cinnamon is some serious motivation to take the world on like a champ. Now, move that idea to lunchtime and pour a steaming-hot bowl of miso soup over the top of that same buckwheat, and add kombu flakes, black sesame seeds, scallions, and broiled tempeh for a bowl of goodness to take you through a day of the Fast Break. Starting your weekly meal prep by cooking off two or three varieties gives you a food foundation to build on. We'll dive into more of that in Convertible Meals on page 233.

COOKING LIQUIDS

- Low-sodium broth (chicken, beef, vegetable)
- Bone broth
- Miso soup
- Unsweetened nut milks (coconut, cashew, almond)
- Infused water (for every 2 cups liquid, add: 1 teaspoon fresh lime or lemon juice or grated fresh turmeric or ginger; or ½ teaspoon ground ginger, garlic powder, curry powder, saffron threads, or ground cumin)

GRAIN TOPPINGS

- Black and/or white sesame seeds
- Dried blueberries (avoid ones with sulfites)
- Goji berries
- Furikake (Japanese seasoning blends with seaweed—see page 104 to make your own)
- Toasted nuts (pine nuts, slivered almonds, chopped walnuts)
- Crispy onions
- Shredded vegetables
- Microgreens
- Spicy sprouts

The Gluten-Free Super Grain (GFSG) Lineup

Oh beautiful for spacious skies, for amber waves of single-ingredient super grains . . .
Just call them GFSGs for short. Man, there are so many options, it'll blow your mind. Go
past the brown rice and explore some of the other tasty grainies listed here. Before you
cook any of these options, make sure you give them a good cleaning. You can find them all
online and many of them in your local grocery store.

Amaranth: This gluten-free grain was a major source of nutrition for the Aztecs and can
be traced back to over eight thousand years ago. It can grow in the harshest conditions
(Amaranth a survivor, I'm not gon' give up!) and offers about 5 grams of protein and
2 grams of fat per ½ cup cooked serving. It's got anti-inflammatory, digestion-boost-
ing, cholesterol-lowering, and weight-loss accelerating powers up the ying-yang, but
it's especially helpful if you're trying to build muscle because it's rich in the amino acid
lysine, which athletes often use as a protein supplement. Amaranth is also a great source
of folate, so if you're preggers or thinking about making a baby, it's a good idea to add it
to your daily rep since it helps to stimulate healthy new cells—which we could all use. Its
nutty flavor makes it a great candidate for a warm or cold breakfast cereal, "rice" pudding, or use in baked goods. It also breaks down easily and can be used to thicken stews,
chili, and gumbo. Now get yo' self summa that!

Black Rice: While you may be familiar with the nutrient power of brown rice, an even
stronger nutritional contender is black rice, also known as Forbidden Rice. It used to be
reserved only for Chinese royalty, but now it's available everywhere. Black rice provides
more fiber, iron, and protein, and it's what I call super rich—gluten-free, packed full of
more antioxidants than any other rice, with anti-inflammatory power that can prevent
weight gain, and detoxifying properties. Plus, it's got 8.5 grams of protein and 5 grams of
fiber per ½ cup cooked serving! It looks gorgeous on a plate when it's paired with colorful
veggies and sauces, and adds an exotic somethin'-somethin' to your dishes. You can use
this delicious rice in recipes and in convertible meal compositions.

Quinoa and Kaniwa: These two ancient grains are actually seeds and are part of the
same family. You know about quinoa because it's shown up in a major way across the
country over the past several years—everywhere from natural foods stores to delis to
Michelin-star restaurants. But do you know about quinoa's cute little sister, kaniwa?

Kaniwa is half the size of quinoa and cooks more quickly. Both are a great source of plant protein, amino acids, and fat—plus, they're high in iron (who says you need meat for protein and iron?). They're gluten-free and go from breakfast to dinner and snacks in between, and are great in sweet or savory preparations. Use them to provide a fun bite and some "heartiness" to your meals.

Buckwheat: Don't let the word *wheat* fool you. Buckwheat is neither wheat nor grain. Just like quinoa and kaniwa, the edible part of buckwheat is a seed that's full of trace minerals and is naturally gluten-free. Buckwheat and buckwheat flour make delicious gluten-free dishes, including waffles that are to die for and aren't filled with garbage like many of the white rice–based varieties of gluten-free flour. You can use buckwheat in stuffing and pilafs, and as a breakfast cereal. I grew up on buckwheat in Egypt; my mom would steep it in milk and add cinnamon, walnuts, and shredded coconut. It's thebomb.com!

Look for super grains in the bulk aisle of your favorite grocery store. That way, you can try a variety in smaller quantities and see which ones you like best. But keep them stored in airtight containers so you don't get uninvited guests nesting in there.

Millet: Instead of a box of chocolate for Valentine's Day, you might want to make your sweetheart a bowl of millet. It's one of the best grains for heart health since it's rich in magnesium, which helps reduce blood pressure and the risk of heart attack or stroke. It's also an awesome source of potassium, which is important for regulating blood pressure.

Sorghum: Chances are, you're probably not as familiar with the whole form of sorghum as you are with the syrup, but lemme tell ya, you're going to want to add this to your repertoire after you read this. Unlike some of its grainy sisters, sorghum gets to hold on to all its outer layers, so it retains a lot of nutrients, making it super rich in antioxidants. Sorghum is also linked with lowering cholesterol, inhibiting cancerous tumor growth, and helping to maintain a healthy blood sugar level. That is chew-worthy.

Teff: It might sound funny, but this grain is legit. It's supercharged and offers a tremendous source of energy with relatively low calories. Teff has a higher nutrient content than wheat and is more easily digested. Plus, it provides calcium, fiber, protein, and antioxidants! Why aren't you already eating this rockin', delicious food?

More Supercharged Grains for Your Brain

While these single-ingredient super grains aren't gluten-free, they still make great choices for people who don't have gluten sensitivities. If you're not sure you fall into that category, you can easily get tested. Many times, even people who have a gluten intolerance can break down these ancient grains.

Farro: This is one of my faves. It has one of the highest fiber contents of all its sisters, at 8 grams per ½ cup cooked serving, and packs about 40 milligrams of calcium and over ten other minerals in the same half cup. It's easy to digest, with a great nutty, chewy flavor. It's super sturdy, holding up to my favorite breakfast cereal dishes, steeped in coconut milk with slivered almonds and unsweetened shredded coconut, and can be used to make one of my loves, farro risotto (aka farrotto). It's also perfect in cold, marinated salads because it won't easily get soft and mushy when dressed. Pasta made from farro flour is one of the best I've ever tasted. With all these bennies, I predict that farro will soon become your jam.

Kamut: One of the ancient grain wonders of the world, kamut (aka Khorasan wheat) is making a comeback. It's known for its firm texture and nutty-buttery taste, likely because it has more fat than other forms of wheat. It's referred to as a "high-energy" super grain because of its nutritional profile, clocking in at 2 grams of fat and a whopping 11 grams of protein per ½ cup cooked serving, with high percentages of magnesium, zinc, and selenium, helping your body arm itself against colds and feeling run-down. Kamut's amino acid profile is off the charts. Sometimes called Pharaoh's wheat, the story behind kamut is that Noah saved this grain on the ark. In the modern day, it adds complexity and a firm texture to dishes. While it does technically contain gluten, many people who are gluten sensitive can tolerate kamut.

Barley: I affectionately refer to barley as the "pedestrian super grain" because it's been around the block forever and a day, and it's about as versatile as it gets when it comes to making an appearance on your nutritionally sound plate. With about 7 grams of protein and 10 grams of fiber in 1 cup cooked, barley is lower in calories than most of its cousins yet higher in fiber. It has a clean, mild flavor that fits in nicely with all your *forkin'* good options. A big benefit of the fiber in barley is beta-glucan, a substance that binds to toxins and pushes them through your system to be eliminated. Think of it as a cowboy with a lasso, capturing the bad stuff in your intestines and herding it out of your body! Now that's what I call a clean-eating grain.

Freekeh: This young wheat grain could be called a "super freekeh" for the many nutritional boosts it provides. While it's often sold as a cracked grain to reduce the cooking time, it retains all the rich nutritional benefits of its whole form. It has a nutty flavor and appealing texture, and was a staple in my upbringing. We used it as a tasty stuffing mixed with currants, chopped walnuts, onions, and celery.

AMAZING GRAINS

Grains are, for the most part, the seeds of grasses. The beautiful thing is that when you sprout a grain, it generates new life. Sprouted grains pack generous amounts of B vitamins, vitamin C, folate, fiber, omega-3s, protein, and EAAs. They also tend to be easier to digest, and people with grain allergies can usually stomach them, too. When sprouted, grains are lower on the glycemic index, which is good news for maintaining healthy blood sugar levels. You'll find them popping up in everything from tortillas to sliced bread to pizza crusts to pasta and good ol' sprouted flour. It's a shoot show.

KANIWA AND FRESH HERB TABBOULI

Tabbouli is one of those salads that feels substantial because it has a single-ingredient grain, but it's also full of fresh flavor, herbage, and just the right amount of raw red onion where you don't feel like your breath might knock someone over. Made from kaniwa, quinoa's cute little sister, this dish is great for parties or picnics, as it holds up well. I grew up on this tabbouli, so it takes me back to my happy place. I hope it does for you, too.

INGREDIENTS

1 cup kaniwa or quinoa

1 teaspoon sea salt, plus more for the water

2 medium tomatoes, seeded and finely chopped

½ English cucumber, finely chopped

1 cup minced fresh parsley leaves

¼ cup minced fresh mint leaves

2 tablespoons finely chopped red onion

3 tablespoons extra-virgin olive oil

1 teaspoon finely chopped lemon zest

2 tablespoons fresh lemon juice

DIRECTIONS

1) Rinse the kaniwa thoroughly. Bring 2 cups salted water to a boil in a medium saucepan. Add the kaniwa and reduce the heat to low. Cook for 15 to 20 minutes, until tender. Let cool thoroughly, about 1 hour.

2) In a medium bowl, combine the tomatoes, cucumber, parsley, mint, and onion. Add the cooled kaniwa and toss together.

3) In a small bowl, whisk together the olive oil, lemon zest, lemon juice, and salt. Pour the mixture over kaniwa and veggies and toss until well incorporated. Serve chilled or at room temperature.

WILD MUSHROOM AMARANTH WITH COLORFUL CAULIFLOWER

WILD MUSHROOM STOCK

2 tablespoons extra-virgin olive oil

2 shallots, minced

1 pound assorted wild mushrooms (porcini, shiitakes, creminis, portobellos), cleaned with Eat Cleaner Wipes, or wiped with a damp paper towel, stems trimmed, and coarsely chopped

¼ cup dry cooking sherry

4 cups low-sodium vegetable broth

1 cup fresh coarsely chopped parsley leaves

Sea salt and cracked black pepper

AMARANTH

2 tablespoons raw coconut oil

¼ cup minced shallots

2 cups uncooked amaranth

Sea salt and cracked black pepper

2 cups chopped assorted cauliflower (purple, green, orange, white), steamed or pan-roasted

2 teaspoons extra-virgin olive oil

A sprinkle of grated pecorino cheese (optional)

DIRECTIONS

1) MAKE THE STOCK: In a large sauté pan, heat the olive oil over medium-high heat. Add the shallots and sauté until translucent, about 2 minutes.

2) Increase the heat to high, add the mushrooms, and sauté tender, about 3 minutes. Add the sherry and stir to deglaze the pan. Stir in the broth and heat until the mixture is hot. Puree the mixture directly in the pot with an immersion blender (or carefully transfer it to a regular blender and puree). Add the parsley, salt, and pepper and puree until smooth.

3) Transfer 4 cups of the stock to a medium saucepan, bring to a boil over high heat, then immediately reduce the heat to maintain simmer.

4) MAKE THE AMARANTH: In a large saucepan or stockpot, melt the coconut oil over medium-high heat. Add the shallots and sauté until translucent, about 2 minutes. Add the amaranth and stir until the grains are coated with the oil and begin to lightly toast, about 1 minute.

5) Add ½ cup of the simmering mushroom stock and reduce the heat to medium low. Cook, stirring continuously, until most of the liquid has been absorbed. Continue adding the stock ½ cup at a time and cooking until it has been absorbed and the amaranth is tender but still slightly al dente, about 20 minutes. Season with salt and cracked black pepper.

6) Spoon the amaranth into bowls and top with cauliflower, a drizzle of good quality extra-virgin olive oil, and some grated pecorino, if desired.

QUINOA BREAKFAST BAKE WITH APPLES AND DATES

INGREDIENTS

Nonstick olive or coconut oil cooking spray

1½ cups uncooked red or white quinoa

½ teaspoon sea salt

½ cup egg whites

⅓ cup unsweetened full fat canned coconut milk

1 teaspoon granulated stevia

1 teaspoon pure vanilla extract

1 tablespoon ground cinnamon

4 dates, pitted and finely diced

1 medium apple, cored and finely diced

2 tablespoons plus two teaspoons natural almond butter (or sunflower seed butter, for a nut-free option)

DIRECTIONS

1) Preheat the oven to 375°F. Spray an 8-inch baking dish with cooking spray.

2) In a medium saucepan, bring 3 cups water to a boil. Add the quinoa and sea salt. Simmer for about 20 minutes, or until quinoa is cooked and the water has been completely absorbed. Transfer the quinoa to a large bowl and let cool.

3) In a small bowl, whisk together the egg whites, coconut milk, stevia, vanilla, and cinnamon until thoroughly combined.

4) Add the egg mixture to the cooled quinoa. Add the dates and apple and stir with a large spoon to combine. Pour the mixture into the prepared baking dish and level the top with a spatula. Bake for 20 to 25 minutes, until set and golden.

5) Let cool completely, then cut into 8 squares. Serve with 1 teaspoon of soft almond butter per square.

CHICKEN SAUSAGE, SPELT, AND PEPPER SKILLET

This is the ultimate, colorful one-pot meal that makes everyone flock to the kitchen when it's cooking.

INGREDIENTS

2 tablespoons raw coconut oil

2 garlic cloves, minced

1 medium red onion, finely diced

1 teaspoon chili powder

1½ to 2 pounds raw chicken sausage, chopped into ½-inch chunks, casings removed

1 cup uncooked spelt

2 cups low-sodium chicken broth

1 medium bell pepper, thinly sliced

2 cups sliced stemmed cremini (baby bella) mushrooms

2 (14.5-ounce) cans diced tomatoes, with their juices

2 teaspoons dried oregano

DIRECTIONS

1) Preheat the oven to 400°F.

2) In a heavy cast-iron or other ovenproof skillet, melt the coconut oil over medium heat. Add the garlic, onion, and chili powder and cook until the onion is translucent, about 2 minutes. Add the chicken sausage and cook for 6 to 8 minutes, until browned.

3) Add the spelt and broth. Reduce the heat to medium and cook for about 5 minutes.

4) Add the bell pepper, mushrooms, tomatoes with their juices, and oregano. Transfer the skillet to the oven and bake for 1 hour, or until the vegetables and spelt are tender and liquid is absorbed. Spoon skillet mixture into a bowl and feel the goodness.

MEDMEX STUFFED PEPPERS

STUFFED PEPPERS

6 large bell peppers

2 tablespoons raw coconut oil

2 garlic cloves, crushed

1 shallot, finely minced

1 pound ground turkey or chicken (see Notes)

½ cup quinoa, rinsed

1 cup lentils, rinsed

1 tablespoon tomato paste

1 cup low-sodium vegetable broth

½ teaspoon ground coriander

½ teaspoon ground cumin

½ teaspoon ground cinnamon

1 teaspoon Himalayan pink salt

½ teaspoon black pepper

MEDMEX TOMATO SAUCE

2 tablespoons tomato paste plus 1½ cup low-sodium vegetable broth

1 teaspoon raw coconut oil, room temperature

½ teaspoon black pepper

½ teaspoon chipotle chili flakes

½ teaspoon Himalayan pink salt

TOPPING

2 tablespoons crumbled sheep's-milk feta cheese

1 tablespoon plus 1 teaspoon minced fresh dill or parsley (optional)

DIRECTIONS

1) Preheat the oven to 400°F.

2) PREPARE THE PEPPERS AND FILLING: Cut the top ½ inch off each bell pepper and remove the seeds and ribs. Set the peppers and their tops aside.

3) In a large nonstick skillet, melt the coconut oil over medium heat. Add the garlic and shallot and cook, stirring, until translucent, 3 to 4 minutes.

4) Add the ground turkey, quinoa, lentils, tomato paste, broth, coriander, cumin, cinnamon, salt, and black pepper. Cook the filling until most of the liquid has been absorbed, 15 to 20 minutes.

5) MAKE THE MEDMEX SAUCE: Meanwhile, in a separate medium saucepan, whisk together all the ingredients for the MedMex sauce until smooth. Bring to a simmer over low heat and cook until reduced by about half, about 12–15 minutes.

6) Stand the peppers upright in an 8-inch baking dish. Spoon the filling into the peppers, filling them three-quarters full, and place the tops back on. Cover with aluminum foil and bake until the filling is thoroughly cooked, 25 to 30 minutes.

7) Spoon the MedMex sauce over the top and finish by sprinkling evenly with the feta. Garnish with dill or parsley, if desired, and serve.

NOTES: For a vegan swap, replace the ground turkey with tempeh or increase the quinoa to 1 cup. You can also slice the peppers in half lengthwise into boats and fill them.

BUCKWHEAT BREAKFAST BOWL

In Egypt, we didn't have boxed cereal, so this was our morning wake-up call. There was nothing better than the smell of the buckwheat simmering, coconut and cinnamon wafting through the air. Despite the name, there's no wheat in here, so it's gluten-free. It's also referred to as groats. This comes together in a flash if you precook the buckwheat in the rice cooker, and the best part is, you can eat it hot or cold.

INGREDIENTS

1 cup uncooked buckwheat, rinsed

2 cups homemade almond milk

1 teaspoon ground cinnamon

4 dates, pitted and finely chopped

TOPPINGS

2 tablespoons unsweetened shredded coconut

2 tablespoons dried currants

2 tablespoons walnuts, crushed

Ground cinnamon

DIRECTIONS

1) In a medium saucepan, combine the buckwheat and 2 cups water and cook until tender, about 30 minutes.

2) In a large saucepan, bring the milk to a boil. Reduce the heat to medium-low and add the cooked buckwheat, cinnamon, and dates. Cook for 10 to 15 minutes, until the milk has somewhat reduced and the mixture has thickened.

3) For each serving, scoop ½ cup of the steeped buckwheat into a bowl and pour ¼ cup of the milk over it. Top with a spoonful of shredded coconut, some currants and walnuts, and a pinch of cinnamon. Delishness!

NO-BAKE OATMEAL PEANUT BUTTER CHOCOLATE CHIP COOKIES

When we shot the photos for this book, everyone went a little cray over the no-bakes. I mean, what's not to love? No baking means less time to your mouth. And all the ingredients just feel so homey and happy together. I think you're never going to want to run out of these in your home.

INGREDIENTS

½ cup canned unsweetened full fat coconut milk

½ cup plus 2 tablespoons natural creamy peanut butter (or sunflower seed butter, for a nut-free option), at room temperature

2 tablespoons raw coconut oil

2 teaspoons granulated stevia or monkfruit sweetener

1 teaspoon pure vanilla extract

¼ teaspoon Himalayan pink salt

3 cups quick-cooking oats

½ cup no-sugar-added dark chocolate chips

DIRECTIONS

1) Line a baking sheet with parchment paper, wax paper, or a silicone mat.

2) In a large bowl, whisk together the coconut milk, ½ cup of the peanut butter, and ½ cup water until smooth. Add the coconut oil, stevia, vanilla, and salt and mix until smooth.

3) Using a spatula, fold in the oats, making sure all the oats are well soaked. Let sit for about 10 minutes, until the mixture becomes firm. Fold in the chocolate chips and mix them with a spatula to evenly distribute.

4) Using an ice cream scoop, portion cookies onto the prepared baking sheet, spacing them about 2 inches apart, and press down lightly to flatten them.

5) In a small bowl, whisk together the remaining 2 tablespoons peanut butter and ½ teaspoon water. Drizzle the peanut butter over the tops of the cookies and let set at room temperature, about 15 minutes. Store wrapped in parchment paper to keep them fresh up to a week.

FAT
FILLERS

If there's a word that strikes fear into the heart, it's *fat*. But repeat after me:

"Fat is not a four-letter word."

"Good fat will not make me fat."

"I need fat in my life."

"Fat is phat." (pretty hot and tempting)

Good fat is the friend that makes the party come to life. You need it to get fit.

There was a period of time, which you'll probably recall or at least have a vague recollection of (circa 1990), when we were told to diligently look for nonfat or at least low-fat options. We were munching on nonfat SnackWell's and reduced-fat Oreos with wild abandon, thinking we were outsmarting Mother Nature and getting to eat whatever we wanted because, well, we weren't eating fat. We were equating an absence of fat with an absence of calories, and needless to say, we got a helluva lot fatter. We went from a national obesity rate of 12 to 14 percent to about double that in the span of a decade. Why? When you take out fat, you have to replace the missing flavor and texture with something—and usually, that "something" is sugar or some type of refined starch. You digest these refined sugars and starches like a brush fire, and that's what sets off spikes in your blood sugar and insulin production, and makes your fun fat pockets want to store all that for winter.

> Good fat is the friend that makes the party come to life.

So you could say the whole low-fat craze is exactly what got us into this fat mess to begin with.

Starting this moment, we're going to retrain our brains to understand that just as much as we need carbohydrates and protein, we need fat—to the tune of 25 to 35 percent of our total daily caloric intake. That's no small amount. Once your brain is on board, your tongue will happily follow suit.

Does that mean we should go eat a side of bacon with fries cooked in duck fat every day? Ummm, no.

What we're after is the type and quantity of fat that counts and the right timing for using fat fillers in your everyday eating plan. This will help put your body into a state of burning more fat instead of turning to that glucose for a quick energy fix first. Fat can also help you shed unwanted pounds by keeping you consistently satiated, and because of that, the fat filler strategy helps to get you through to the next meal. It's the key to keeping you satiated and your blood sugar stable so that you don't binge or, worse, walk around like a zombie in a hangry stupor all day. "Good" fat, the kind that actually lowers your cholesterol, helps with brain function, and balances hormones, is an essential part of weight control.

The 411 on Fats

The goal here is to skim *saturated* fat, the fat that clogs your arteries and stresses your heart, which mostly comes from meat and other animal products. It can wreak havoc on your heart health and, quite frankly, your booty. This is why our Fast Break strategy is so important.

Quality plant-based fats and wild-caught fatty seafood in the right amounts hit the satiety button like an erogenous zone.

HEALTHY FATS TO ENJOY THE *FORKIN'* GOOD WAY:

Whole avocados

Sunflower seeds

Flaxseed

Chia seeds

Hemp seeds

Coconut

Walnuts

Almonds

Cashews

Macadamia nuts

Nut butters

Sunflower seed butter

Wild-caught seafood (salmon, mackerel, sardines)

GOOD-QUALITY OILS (BESIDES THE OBVIOUS EXTRA-VIRGIN OLIVE OIL):

Walnut oil

Sesame oil

Coconut oil

Black seed oil

Hemp oil

Avocado oil

MCT oil

Flax oil

For high-heat cooking, use oils with a high smoking point like coconut, sesame, and grapeseed oils. Save the extra-virgin olive oil for low-heat cooking, dressings, and uncooked dishes.

FOR THE LOVE OF AVOCADOS

The mild, creamy flavor of avocados makes them perfect for many dishes, whether it be in your favorite guacamole recipe, on wraps, or blended into smoothies, soups, or baked goods—even desserts—and they go especially well with chocolate!

They contain more potassium than bananas, which is essential for muscle growth and organ function, and they are full of essential vitamins like C, E, K and antioxidants that keep the immune system strong. The flesh is also full of healthy monounsaturated fats that won't raise your cholesterol levels. Plus, avocados make everything taste better! Who are we kidding—just add a little salt and pepper and eat it right out of the skin.

MONOUNSATURATED FATS

WHY? With one saturated carbon bond, these fats can help reduce bad cholesterol and help maintain healthy cells.

WHERE? Look for them in their whole form, preferably expeller- or cold-pressed to preserve the nutrient content and avoid the use of chemicals in processing. Cold-pressing oils also helps to preserve their delicate flavors, which makes a cold-pressed olive oil a precious gift from heaven! Heat and the use of hexane in processing destroy enzymes and the inherent health benefits of the oil.

Whole olives and olive oil
Avocados and avocado oil
Nuts and nut oils (almond, peanut, pecans)
Seeds and seed oils (pumpkin, sesame, safflower)

POLYUNSATURATED FATS

WHY? These fats are often filled with omega-3s, which are so important for the body because it can't produce them on its own.

WHERE? Best enjoyed eaten in their whole, wild-caught forms for seafood, as farm-raised varieties can be disproportionately higher in inflammatory omega-6s. Although your body needs omega-6s, too, they're usually easier to obtain than omega-3s.

Flaxseeds and flax oil
Fatty fish (salmon, mackerel, sardines)
Walnuts

FATS TO ENJOY IN SMALL AMOUNTS

WHY? Because these are considered saturated fats, the recommendation from the American Heart Association is to limit their consumption to 5 to 6 percent of total calories.

WHERE? Look for them in their natural forms and as ingredients in prepared foods or used at your favorite restaurant. Don't be afraid to ask for the ingredient list!

Full-fat milk products, including cheeses
Red meat, bacon, lunch meats, and other fatty cuts
Butter
Lard
Palm oil

FATS TO AVOID LIKE YOUR LIFE DEPENDS ON IT

WHY? They raise LDL ("bad") cholesterol levels, contributing to heart disease, stroke, and insulin resistance; and create a backlash of inflammation.

WHERE? Aside from their obvious form in a tub, stick, or bottle, look for them in most packaged baked goods, snack foods, cookies, crackers, and fried foods.

Hydrogenated and partially hydrogenated oils (aka trans fats)
Margarine (trans fat)
Soybean oil (most is GMO and pesticide-laden)
Corn oil (ditto soybean oil)

In a League of Its Own: Coconut

Never has a nut caused so much controversy. Is it healthy? Should you avoid it? Should anyone ever wear a coconut bra? Yes, no, and no, in that order.

The hotly contested coconut fat debate. Here's the dealio:

While it is high in saturated fat, coconut and products derived from it like coconut oil contain so many bennies, it legitimately earns its superfood status. About half of the saturated fat it contains is made of lauric acid, which is a potent antimicrobial that'll knock bacteria, viruses, and fungi onto their behinds and help you fight infection. It also contains a good amount of medium-chain triglycerides (MCTs), which have been linked with boosting weight loss, helping to rev your metabolism, and feeding your brain so you feel like a smart, sexy superhero. Coconut oil can also lower cholesterol and has a high smoking point that makes it safer to use when cooking with high heat. Just avoid any kind of coconut oil with "hydrogenated" or "partially hydrogenated" on the label. Add a tablespoon to your tea or coffee in the morning to kick-start that awesomely creative, resourceful mind of yours. Coconut butter is made with the meat of the coconut, so feel free to spread some of that love like you would peanut or almond butter.

A great way to enjoy coconut is in Chocolate Coconutter Dip (page 194). It makes the perfect dip for apple or pear slices, strawberries, or a spoon. Enjoy a couple of tablespoons of this as a fat filler snack, and do a happy dance on your way to Flavorville on the daily.

Before you go sneaking off to dredge your T-bone in bacon grease, let me just remind you that not all fat is created equal, so I want to help you balance your monounsaturated fatty acids (MUFAs) and prioritize them. Baked goods and mashes are where you tend to find a lot of heaviness. You can take out a ton of butter and shortening by swapping in fruit and veggie purees in their place. Beets, sweet potato, butternut squash, cauliflower, and pumpkin are a few of my tried-and-true ones. These purees have the density and moisture to perform the same way butter does in these dishes. I've used them in cupcakes, cookies, breads—even my decadent mocha chocolate cake, which was a winner on *Recipe Rehab* (see below).

WHAT THE FORK?

The Emmy-nominated show, *Recipe Rehab*, where I was a featured chef, revolved around the concept that every family favorite could be enjoyed more healthfully. Some of the recipes we saw were off the charts in terms of sugar, saturated fat, and empty calories. I once over-hauled a mac 'n' cheese recipe that had 80 grams of saturated fat per serving. Holy artery-clogging noo-dles, Batman!

Back to that mocha chocolate cake I mentioned: Originally, the recipe for Aunt Alice's Chocolate Cake called for 2½ cups powdered sugar, 1 cup vegetable oil, 2 cups granulated sugar, and ¾ cup whole milk. I took out *all* the sugar, *all* the oil, and the whole milk. Gone. Like, none. I replaced them with 1 cup pureed canned beets and 1 cup xylitol, a calorie-free sugar alcohol used as a sweetener. The kicker was the kids in the family mixed the beets in them-selves and still picked my cake as the winner—and saved themselves over 3000 calories.

Cauliflower can add body to frosting and fillings, while butternut squash and pump-kin are great complements to spiced cakes and cookies. These purees also make a great creamy center for desserts like filled crepes and substitute for buttercream when blended with coconut butter, for example. So now you get to enjoy your birthday cake and eat it guiltlessly, too.

Now what other F words do you associate fat with?

| Fun | Flavorful | Fantastic | Fabulous | Fulfilling |

That's what I thought!

You're hangry at the office and everyone is pissing you off. Then the vending machine starts seducing you like the siren's song . . . *come closer, pick the M&M's, eat me* . . . or you're heading home after a long meeting where you didn't get to eat your fat filler snack and you see the golden arches glimmering in the distance. There's a sign that read, "Hey, gorgeous, we're so excited to see you! Just pull up to the drive-thru and order whatever you want! You're Lovin' It."

Unless you're superhuman, will-power won't do ANYTHING for you right now. It's time to armor up. Following are a few snacks you can keep in your bag, car, briefcase, or glove compartment that will hold up for the distance. And the best part is, you can have up to two of these fat fillers in between meals. One more happy dance!

- Fill snack bags with homemade trail mix that includes raw almonds, coconut flakes, hemp hearts, and dried apples for the perfect fat filler.
- Keep a few pouches of nut butter handy.
- Whip up a batch of Garlic and Rosemary Baked Olives (page 40) and store them in a glass jar for easy, between-meal snacking.
- Bag up single-serving portions of unsalted seeds and nuts, like sunflower seeds, cashews, pistachios, and pumpkin seeds.
- Feel free to enjoy a Marbled Tahini Fudge Bar (page 197) between meals—they're totally addictive, in a good way

THE REAL DISH RANCH DRESSING

Let's face it—everything tastes better with ranch dressing, including chicken wings, veggies, and, well, salad. Let's just not drown our food in it. This serves as a good fat filler option, great for skinny dippin' with raw veggies. The fresh dill and chives make this dressing extra fresh.

INGREDIENTS

1 cup coconut oil mayonnaise (no fillers; vegan options abound)

3 tablespoons unsweetened homemade almond milk

Juice of 1 small lemon

1 teaspoon Dijon mustard

2 tablespoons minced fresh chives

1 tablespoon onion powder

1 tablespoon garlic powder

2 teaspoons minced fresh dill

½ teaspoon smoked paprika

½ teaspoon sea salt

½ teaspoon ground white pepper

DIRECTIONS

1) In a medium bowl, whisk together the mayonnaise, almond milk, lemon juice, and mustard. Add the chives, onion powder, garlic powder, dill, paprika, salt, and white pepper and whisk together until uniform.

2) Store in an airtight container or mason jar in the refrigerator for up to a month.

SPINACH AND MUSHROOM FRITTATA CUPS

INGREDIENTS

2 tablespoons ghee (clarified butter) or raw coconut oil

2 tablespoons chopped shallot

½ cup finely chopped cremini (baby bella) mushrooms

1½ cups fresh chopped spinach

2 tablespoons finely diced red bell pepper

2 large eggs

1 cup egg whites

¼ cup unsweetened homemade almond milk

1½ teaspoons baking powder

½ teaspoon smoked sea salt

1 teaspoon freshly ground black pepper

¼ cup diced fresh mozzarella cheese

DIRECTIONS

1) Preheat the oven to 400°F. Grease six wells of a muffin tin with a little coconut oil or line them with paper liners.

2) In a large skillet, melt 1 tablespoon of ghee over medium heat. Add the shallot and sauté until soft, about 1 minute. Add the red bell pepper and mushrooms and cook until soft, 3 to 4 minutes. Add the spinach and cook until just wilted, about 1 minute. Remove from the heat and transfer to a paper towel, squeezing off excess moisture.

3) In a small bowl, whisk together the eggs, egg whites, almond milk, baking powder, remaining 1 tablespoon ghee, salt, and pepper until frothy.

4) Divide the spinach mixture evenly among the prepared muffin cups. Pour the egg mixture into each cup, filling them two-thirds full, then evenly distribute the mozzarella among each. Bake for 20 to 25 minutes, until the egg is set. Serve warm and store the rest in a sealed container and refrigerate. These make a great meal prep dish, so double the batch and wrap in aluminum foil to pop into the freezer. Just heat them up in the oven or toaster oven when you're ready to enjoy.

AVOCADO ANGEL EGGS

INGREDIENTS

12 hard-boiled large eggs, peeled

2 ripe avocados

2 tablespoons fresh lemon juice

1 tablespoon Dijon mustard

1 tablespoon fresh parsley

1 teaspoon garlic powder

½ teaspoon ground white pepper

½ teaspoon sea salt

2 tablespoons minced fresh chives

DIRECTIONS

1) Slice each egg in half lengthwise, taking care not to tear the egg whites, and scoop the egg yolks into a medium bowl. Set the egg whites aside.

2) Halve and pit the avocados and scoop flesh into a medium bowl. Add the lemon juice, mustard, parsley, garlic powder, white pepper, and salt.

3) Transfer the mixture to a food processor (set the bowl aside) and pulse until creamy; add a few drops of water if more liquid is needed. Return the mixture to the bowl and stir in the chives.

4) Spoon the avocado mixture into the egg whites. (Alternatively, for a beautiful presentation, transfer the filling to a pastry bag fitted with a decorative tip and pipe it into the egg whites.) Arrange the eggs on a platter and serve or store in a sealed container for when you're ready to munch.

SMOKED SALMON AND CHIVE MOUSSE ON CUCUMBER SLICES

It feels so fancy but it's so easy and versatile to mix into your meals. You could use this salmon mousse to also top an overstuffed baked sweet potato, in a convertible bowl, or as an egg topper.

INGREDIENTS

4 ounces smoked wild-caught salmon

¾ cup plain full-fat Greek yogurt

1 tablespoon coarsely chopped fresh dill

2 teaspoons fresh minced chives, plus more for garnish

½ teaspoon lemon zest

1 tablespoon fresh lemon juice

½ teaspoon smoked sea salt

1 English cucumber, cut into ¼-inch-thick rounds

DIRECTIONS

1) In a food processor, combine the smoked salmon and yogurt. Pulse until well incorporated and creamy. Add the dill, chives, lemon zest, lemon juice, and salt. Pulse for 30 seconds to combine.

2) Arrange the cucumber slices on a platter. Spoon the salmon mixture onto the cucumber slices. (Alternatively, transfer the salmon mixture to a pastry bag and swirl it onto the cucumber.)

SOFIA'S SEAFOOD SALAD–STUFFED AVOCADOS

Before you say "ew," so did she. My daughter was okay with tuna, but turned her nose up at sardines and mackerel. But as soon as she tried these seafood salad–stuffed avos, she became a believer. We're gonna expand your view on canned fish, too, because quite frankly, tuna isn't the only great catch in town. Sardines and mackerel make for an omega-3-rich combo, and they tend to be much lower in mercury, so get to know and love these two fatty friends.

INGREDIENTS

2 very ripe medium avocados

1 tablespoon Dijon mustard

1 teaspoon grated lemon zest

2 tablespoons fresh lemon juice

1 tablespoon plus 1 teaspoon finely chopped fresh dill leaves

2 tablespoons finely chopped fresh chives

1 teaspoon each sea salt and freshly ground black pepper; more as needed

2 (3.75- to 4.375-ounce) cans wild-caught skinless, boneless sardines, drained

2 (4.375-ounce) cans wild-caught skinless, boneless mackerel, drained

2 celery stalks, finely chopped

2 tablespoons pine nuts, toasted (see Note)

DIRECTIONS

1) Halve and pit the avocados and scoop most of the flesh into a large bowl, leaving a border around the edge and keeping the avocado skins intact. Set the skins aside. Add the mustard, lemon zest, lemon juice, 1 tablespoon of the dill, the chives, salt, and pepper and whisk until smooth. Add the sardines, mackerel, celery, and 1½ tablespoons of the pine nuts. Using the back of a fork, break up the fish and mix until all the ingredients are well incorporated. Taste and adjust the salt and pepper.

2) Spoon the seafood salad mixture into the avocado skins. Top each with a few of the remaining pine nuts, remaining dill, and a twist of pepper.

NOTE: To toast pine nuts, put them in a small dry skillet and toast over medium heat for 5 minutes, shaking the pan regularly to avoid burning.

MAKES 4 SERVINGS

SAUCY ITALIAN STUFFED MUSHROOMS (AND ANYTHING ELSE YOU WANNA STUFF)

When I was growing up, my family was very fond of stuffed things: stuffed grape leaves, stuffed peppers, stuffed cabbage, stuffed zucchini, to name a few. But we didn't have mushrooms—the ultimate umami mami—so we're making up for lost time. These are definitely hearty enough to serve as an entrée, especially when they've got a green veg or salad on the side to brighten them up.

INGREDIENTS

16 large cremini (baby bella) mushrooms

½ red bell pepper, coarsely chopped

2 garlic cloves

2 tablespoons fresh parsley

2 tablespoons extra-virgin olive oil

2 tablespoons raw coconut oil or extra-virgin olive oil

1 medium yellow onion, minced

1 pound uncooked chicken sausage, casings removed (see Note)

DIRECTIONS

1) Preheat the oven to 375°F. Line a baking sheet with parchment paper or a silicone baking mat.

2) Stem the mushrooms; put the stems in a food processor and set the caps aside in a bowl. Add the bell pepper, garlic, parsley, and olive oil to the food processor and pulse until finely chopped. Set aside.

3) In a large skillet, melt 1 tablespoon of the coconut oil over medium heat. Add the onion and cook until translucent, about 8 minutes. Add the sausage and sauté, breaking up the meat with tongs or the back of a spoon as it cooks, for about 10 minutes.

4) Add the mushroom mixture, flaxseed, salt, and black pepper to the skillet and cook for another 3 to 4 minutes, until all the ingredients mesh together nicely. Remove from the heat.

(continued)

190   EAT LIKE YOU GIVE A FORK

⅓ cup ground flaxseed

1 teaspoon sea salt

1 teaspoon freshly ground black pepper

Nonstick olive or coconut oil cooking spray

1 cup prepared arrabbiata sauce (see page 131)

¼ cup freshly grated pecorino (optional)

5) Mist each mushroom cap with cooking spray, then arrange them rounded-side down on the prepared baking sheet. Fill each one to the top and pack the mixture down with the back of the spoon. Sprinkle a little pecorino over each one and bake for 20 to 25 minutes, until the tops are nice and brown.

6) Serve the mushrooms on a platter with a dollop of arrabbiata sauce on top of each.

NOTES: You can definitely use the same filling for any of the vessels I mentioned in the headnote. Stuff away! For a vegan swap, substitute one 16-ounce package sprouted tofu with 2 teaspoons coconut amino acids for the sausage.

CHOCOLATE CHIP WALNUT BANANA BREAD

The addition of collagen protein adds a nice springiness to this decadent loaf. Leaving the peels on makes this banana bread extra moist and jam-packed with essential nutrients! Trust me, you'll want to double the batch, and maybe add more chocolate.

INGREDIENTS

3 whole bananas, peels on (see page 237)

3 large eggs

3 tablespoons ghee (clarified butter)

1 teaspoon pure vanilla extract

¼ cup unsweetened almond milk

1 cup all-purpose gluten-free flour

¼ cup chopped walnuts

2 heaping tablespoons bone broth collagen protein powder

2 teaspoons granulated stevia

1 teaspoon baking soda

½ teaspoon sea salt

⅓ cup plus 2 tablespoons dark chocolate chips (70% or more unsweetened cacao)

DIRECTIONS

1) Preheat the oven to 375°F. Line a 4-cup loaf pan (8"x 4"x 2½") with parchment paper.

2) In a blender, combine the bananas (still in their peels), eggs, ghee, vanilla, and almond milk and blend until smooth.

3) In a large bowl, stir together the flour, walnuts, protein powder, stevia, baking soda, and salt until evenly combined. Add the banana mixture and stir to incorporate. Fold in ⅓ cup of the chocolate chips. Pour the mixture into the prepared loaf pan, spreading it evenly, and sprinkle the remaining 2 tablespoons chocolate chips on top.

4) Bake for 50 to 55 minutes, until a toothpick inserted into the center comes out clean. Let cool in the pan for 10 to 15 minutes. Slice and serve, or store in a sealed container and refrigerate for up to a week—although there's no way it's making it that long.

CHOCOLATE COCONUTTER DIP

This is a perfect example of a fat filler that, while you're eating it, you won't believe it's guilt-free. So creamy and delish, it's a treat you can look forward to daily in between meals, with fresh sliced apples, pears, or strawberries.

INGREDIENTS

2 cups cashews

¼ cup raw coconut oil (see Note)

2 tablespoons unsweetened cocoa powder

6 drops liquid stevia, or
1 teaspoon granulated stevia

½ teaspoon cinnamon

DIRECTIONS

1) In a large dry skillet, toast the cashews over low heat until lightly golden. Transfer them to a food processor and pulse until broken down into a smooth butter. Add the coconut oil and pulse until smooth and creamy.

2) Add the cocoa powder, stevia, and cinnamon. Pulse until well incorporated. Transfer to a glass jar and store at room temperature for up to a month (if you can get it to last that long).

NOTE: Solid coconut oil works best here. If yours has liquefied, just pour it into a measuring cup and stick it in the fridge until solid.

MARBLED TAHINI FUDGE BARS

Can I be honest? These are my absolute favorite fudge bars ever. If that sounds egocentric, I'm sorry (#notsorry). Just try them, you'll see what I mean. The tahini/fudge combo is, well, very enticing!

INGREDIENTS

1 cup tahini (sesame paste)

⅓ cup raw coconut oil, room temperature

¼ cup pure maple syrup

½ teaspoon sea salt

1 teaspoon pure vanilla extract

¼ cup unsweetened cocoa powder

DIRECTIONS

1) In a medium bowl, whisk together the tahini and coconut oil until smooth. Add the maple syrup, salt, and vanilla and stir until creamy. Divide the mixture evenly between two small bowls. Whisk the cocoa powder into one bowl.

2) Pour the batter without cocoa powder into an 8-inch baking dish. Dollop the cocoa powder portion on top and use a toothpick or the back of a spoon to swirl the two together and create marble effect (do not stir until combined—the swirls should be distinct). Refrigerate in a sealed container for at least 2 hours or up to overnight to harden.

3) Cut the fudge into twelve 2-inch blocks and store in an airtight container in the freezer to keep their firm texture.

STRATEGY 7

BE REAL
DENSE

Oh, my, God, Becky, look at her butt.

Well, not quite that kind of dense.

Getting real dense means making every bite count by eating nutrient-dense foods to turbo boost your vibrancy and vitality. Think about this in cash terms. You get more bang out of your calorie buck with nutritionally dense ingredients that feed you to the core. Investing in foods and super-food add-ons now will give you a hefty ROI on your health down the road. The idea is to "level up" every meal. I call it squeezing the juice out of every meal in order to drench your body in goodness. Do you get the visual?

Leafy greens, seeds, raw foods, spices, and probiotics deliver the most nutrient density, earning the title of "superfoods." As a chef, I've learned that some of the best recipes and meals are where the dense add-ons take the cake. This applies not only for taste and texture purposes, but also for creating the most flavorful meals you can create. A pop, a crunch, a burst of heat, an earthy spice—they can all contribute to the end goal of boosting your basics up a big notch. Because you are no basic b*%ch.

Foods like hemp and black seeds, spices like cinnamon and turmeric, probiotics in cultured and fermented foods, and even natural sweeteners like honey and dates all have a role to play for their health benefits. We'll explore a variety of these superfood add-ons that can boost flavor and texture all while supporting your hot bod.

The fact that they can really transform your meals is a huge bonus. In this strategy, we'll explore some nutrient-dense flavor add-ons that you can try with any recipe or mix in with the Convertible Meals strategy (see page 233). Let me introduce you to the flavor offerings and encourage you to expand your palate and your palette.

Getting Seedy

Turns out, being seedy isn't a bad thing. A few years ago, I was experiencing a lot of stiffness in my fingers when I would wake up in the morning—and it would last for hours. I felt like I had a claw hand, and it was really freaking me out. I thought, I'm way too young to be feeling this rigid after a good night's sleep. When I realized that my hard-core work-out was causing the problem, I started doing some research. My Egyptian heritage led me to this potent form of black cumin decades ago, but recent medical research is revealing mind-boggling reasons to include this seed in your meals. Just 1 to 2 teaspoons a day can make a world of difference. Black seeds have more than one hundred phytochemicals that help your body heal—from relieving asthma and increasing flexibility to lowering blood pressure to aiding in colon health. A great way to enjoy their wonder powers is in a za'atar spice blend (page 207), using it as a dip or crust for proteins. Black seeds have a pretty assertive flavor, almost licorice-like, so a little goes a long way.

OTHER SEEDS TO EXPLORE

- Chia
- Hemp (see page 202)
- Flaxseed
- Black sesame
- Pumpkin
- Sunflower

Aside from topping salads, sautés, and soups with seeds, you can grind them and use them as a substitute for bread crumbs. My son's favorite food in the world is breaded chicken tenders, so I create a crust out of ground pumpkin, flax, and sunflower seeds, then dip chicken strips in a seasoned egg batter, roll them in the seed coating, spray them with nonstick cooking spray, and bake to perfection. It works like a charm, with no junky fillers. They're officially "his" now, but he allowed me to share the recipe with you on page 211.

Be RAWsome

There are three BIG reasons why getting raw is something we should all get behind:

1. **Raw fruits and vegetables deliver pure nutrition, always at the ready to deliver the most potent vitamins, minerals, fibers, and enzymes, which help digestion and build a healthy gut.**
2. **Raw foods require minimal prep, and quickly satisfy your need to munch.**
3. **Raw produce is hydrating and feeds your cellular functions.**

Aim to have one raw meal every day. Eating raw can simply be one salad or one fresh juice or one serving of guacamole a day. You can handle that! You'll find it can greatly contribute to your macronutrient balance for the day, as you use smaller amounts of fat and carbs to add taste and texture to your raw veggies and fruit. The act of eating raw foods is great for your system, keeping things flowin', if you know what I mean.

On a Hemp High

I'm not talking about pot, folks. Well, maybe a little. It's the edible part of the hemp plant, and soon it'll have you wondering, *Where have you been all my life?!* Hemp is an ancient plant, and it is a complete form of protein, fat, and good carbohydrates rolled into one.

Nutty, flavorful hemp seeds and hemp oil are super rich and can improve your skin, bolster cardiovascular health, and slow the aging process. Know that the hemp seeds used to produce hemp milk, protein, oil and other by-products don't contain any significant levels of THC, so don't worry about failing a drug test or getting so high you forget your beet brownies are in the oven.

For vegetarians, hemp can be a fantastic source of the much-needed omega-3 and omega-6 fats in just the right balance. Hemp oil has a fairly assertive flavor profile and is best when blended with another oil like avocado oil or extra-virgin olive oil and whisked together with vinegar to dress greens and other veggies. Hulled hemp seeds (hemp hearts) go nicely on top of just about any dish you want to give a little pop of savory flavor. You can even sub them in for croutons or fried wontons on a salad. Try hemp protein powder in smoothies or protein balls to give them additional superpower. Just avoid heating hemp oil because, ironically, it has a low smoking point and can hydrogenate at high temps.

MIX IT UP SO THAT YOU NEVER GET BORED OR TIRED OF RAW FOOD

1. **GET CRUNCHY.** Now that you are retraining your taste buds, eat as much produce in raw form as possible so that you can really appreciate their pure flavors, such as carrots, celery, cucumber, jicama, sugar snap peas, and bell pepper. It is beyond satisfying to feel the crunch of a tasty bite of carrot or jicama. If someone you love has a texture aversion, chances are they'll eat it raw as long as there's something yummy to dip into.
2. **SKINNY DIP.** Add a big-flavor fat dunker for your veggies to make a quick mini meal. Make-ahead dips like The Real Dish Ranch Dressing (page 181), Roasted Red Pepper Pesto (page 69), and Romesco Sauce (page 39) can double up as a salad dressing, sauce, or protein topper.
3. **SIP YOUR VEGGIES.** One of the easiest ways to slip in a ton of raw veggies is with a cold soup, gazpacho-style (page 80). Add tomatoes, greens, zucchini, peppers, onion, and garlic, season with salt and black pepper, and blend until silky smooth. Or make pure veggie juice blends with a tomato base to keep them easy to sip.
4. **ZOODLE YOUR NOODLE.** By spiralizing veggies like zucchini, beets, and yellow squash, you'll have more fun with their texture. Toss these noodles with spinach pesto and you'll be straight-up raw twirling like a champ (page 76).
5. **FREEZE FRAME.** Blend greens and avocado with fruit to make ice pops. Add nut butter, plain Greek yogurt, or coconut milk to make them creamy, dreamy, and full of protein. It becomes a treat that feels like a cheat. And who doesn't love sin on a stick?

Great Dates

What are the best kinds of dates? The ones you eat, even the kind with the pits.

While I have included many ancient foods in my plan, dates are one of the oldest foods and have been used by healers for centuries. They provide an abundance of health benefits, from dietary fiber and roughage for colon health to potassium, B vitamins, and iron. Just understand that with all that natural shuga, a little date love goes a long way. When used in moderation—think: four whole dates—to add flavor and nutritional benefits, they can be the kind of food that satisfies like only a good date can. Combining them with good fat like nut butters and nut milk helps keep your body's glycemic index from spiking out.

Cinna-mmmm . . .

Cinnamon is my go-to when it comes to yumminess. Its exotic aroma and flavor are just so, so good. We often think of it as a special treat, especially around the holidays, but why shouldn't it be part of your meal planning all the time? Cinnamon is a potent infection fighter, helps repair damaged tissues, acts as an antifungal and anti-inflammatory in the body, and helps control blood sugar. Cinnamon is a must in any effort to improve your metabolism. I use the more potent Ceylon cinnamon in my meal plans and recipes, instead of the more common cassia cinnamon. Add it to your breakfast grains, use it as a topping for protein balls, or stir it into your morning coffee with a spoonful of coconut oil. I'm all about feeling like Christmas every day. Just don't eat it by the spoonful in a Cinnamon Challenge like my friend Glozell (you'll have to YouTube that one).

Tantalizing Turmeric

Turmeric is another of my favorite ancient spices, used for centuries in many parts of the world. It adds a specific earthy taste to just about anything savory. Plus, the rich yellow color of ground turmeric is just gawwwjus! It can be sprinkled into tea or turned into a golden latte; marries beautifully with equal parts cinnamon, nutmeg, and ginger as a seasoning for pork or chicken; and partners perfectly with a spicy blend of cayenne, cumin, coriander seeds, sea salt, and black pepper for a curry (see page 88). Fresh turmeric root lends a completely different, mellow vibe: Grate ½ teaspoon into a cup of hot water with a squeeze of lemon and a dash of cayenne for a yummy detox tea.

It has become a lot easier to find fresh turmeric root, and it's so worth foraging for! In a recent animal study, turmeric was found to boost the plant-based conversion of omega-3s into DHA in the brain. The exciting factor was the percentage of the boost: about 50 percent additional DHA when the diet included turmeric (National Institutes of Health, Fact Sheet for Health Professionals; Omega-3 Fatty Acids). Turmeric is also an impressive ant-inflammatory and has been shown to reduce arthritic pain. Recent studies show that it may also have a cognitive function in the brain, decreasing depression and even slowing the effects of Alzheimer's disease. The active compound is curcumin, and based on research from the National Institutes of Health, consuming turmeric with black pepper can increase the bioavailability of the curcumin to make it a whole lot more useful to your body. It takes turmeric, baby.

Prebiotic Power

We've heard all about the importance of probiotics, but before you get those into your system, you need to spread the fertilizer into that gut garden to help it grow. This can be done with prebiotics, which we can get naturally from foods like onions, garlic, asparagus, and bananas. Get an added boost from chicory root, dandelion, and Jerusalem artichoke. Once you get your pipes nice and clog-free, the right stuff can do its magic. Prebiotics are getting a lot more attention now and were featured as a "trend to watch" in my 6th annual Healthy Food & Beverage Trends report.

Probiotic Punch

"Trust your gut" means more than you can imagine. Often referred to as "the little brain," your gut controls your mood, your ability to absorb nutrients and regulate hormones— and probiotics significantly aid the process. Probiotics are live bacteria that help to keep your health, especially the health of your digestive system, balanced and in check, but their impact goes way beyond that. Just think of probiotics as the pump that keeps things flowin'. Your ability to lose weight and burn fat, the clarity of your skin, your immunity and the ability to ward off colds are all major bennies of a probiotic-rich plan. By the way, when you're hangry, it's your gut in control of whether you will stab someone with your fork or lovingly look into their eyes, so keep your probiotic friends close and your frenemies closer.

You might think of probiotics as something in yogurt or kefir, but they also come from fermented and pickled foods and drinks like kombucha. Some nondairy probiotic-rich foods to dig your fork into include:

- Kimchi
- Sauerkraut
- Pickled veggies
- Sourdough starter

- Kombucha
- Apple cider vinegar
- Fermented black garlic

Since the flavor of these foods can be pretty bold, treat them as a condiment for meats, as a topper for your single-ingredient super-grain bowls, and, in the case of black garlic, as an add-on to dressings, salsa, and guacamole. You'll get to enjoy the benefits of apple cider vinegar with the Real Vitality Tonic (page 47), too. If you start to feel some bloating or discomfort with these foods, this is natural. It just means your body is adjusting to all this gut-boosting goodness. And a little gas never hurt anyone. Remember the kombu trick?

Lifestyles of the Super Rich

I love how food offerings have become so diverse over the years. When I started doing my Healthy Food & Beverage Trends report, I decided a superfoods category was worth creating because everyone was wondering, *What comes after açaí when it comes to antioxidant value and disease-fighting properties?* If you're going to get super rich when it comes to superfoods, a variety of berries, superfruits, and roots work nicely as toppings for your bowls, bakes, stews, soups, salads, and, of course, on their own.

- Maca powder
- Goji berries
- Blueberries
- Pitaya (dragon fruit)
- Açaí
- Tart cherries
- Unsweetened shredded coconut

- Unsweetened cocoa powder
- Matcha/green tea
- Reishi and chaga mushrooms
- Spirulina
- Raw coconut oil

ZA'ATAR WITH BLACK SEEDS (HAB-ET EL BARAKHA)

Za'atar is a delicious spice blend using black cumin seeds (in Arabic hab-et el Barakha, "a small blessing") that you can sprinkle on a wide variety of foods, from roasted veggies to soups and salads. I also love it stirred into extra-virgin olive oil as a dip for veggies and blended into hummus or tahini. It's packed with health benefits, too.

INGREDIENTS

1 tablespoon black cumin seeds

1 tablespoon sesame seeds

2 tablespoons dried thyme

2 tablespoons dried oregano

1 tablespoon ground sumac

1 teaspoon coarse sea salt

1 teaspoon black pepper

DIRECTIONS

In a small dry skillet, toast the cumin seeds and sesame seeds over low heat until fragrant. Do not let the sesame seeds darken in color. Transfer to an airtight container, stir in the thyme, oregano, sumac, salt, and pepper, cover, and store in a cool, dark place.

PUMPKIN SPICE PROTEIN SMOOTHIE

Pumpkin, I love you more than pie. You're rich in fiber, you're low in calories, you're super hydrating, full of antioxidants, you help boost my immunity, you help regulate my blood sugar, you help me feel fuller longer, and you taste amazing in so many ways, like this smoothie.

INGREDIENTS

1 cup unsweetened almond milk, coconut milk, or hemp milk

1 frozen banana, cut in half, peel left on

⅔ cup pure pumpkin puree

½ cup plain Greek yogurt

¼ teaspoon pure vanilla extract

¼ teaspoon pumpkin pie spice

1 teaspoon granulated stevia

½ cup ice

¼ teaspoon ground cinnamon, plus more for garnish

DIRECTIONS

In a blender, combine the almond milk, banana, pumpkin, and yogurt. Blend until smooth. Add the vanilla, pumpkin pie spice, stevia, ice, and cinnamon and blend for 15 seconds. Pour into a glass and top with a sprinkle of cinnamon. Enjoy ice-cold.

LUCCA'S SUPERCHARGED CHICKEN TENDERS WITH TURMERIC AND HONEY DIJON DIPPING SAUCE

This is the way to my son's heart and stomach, with a dense crust that makes me feel like I've done good work as a mom, versus the "food products" you find in the frozen food aisle. Let no one be the wiser.

INGREDIENTS

1 cup egg whites

1 tablespoon coconut amino acids or tamari

1 teaspoon sea salt

½ teaspoon ground white pepper

12 boneless chicken tenders

CRUST

½ cup almond or coconut flour

¼ cup ground flaxseed

2 tablespoons raw hulled pumpkin seeds

1 tablespoon sunflower seeds

1 teaspoon sea salt

½ teaspoon smoked paprika

¼ teaspoon onion powder

Nonstick olive or coconut oil cooking spray

TURMERIC AND HONEY DIJON DIPPING SAUCE

2 tablespoons Dijon mustard

1 tablespoon raw honey

½ teaspoon ground turmeric

½ teaspoon sea salt

DIRECTIONS

1) Preheat the oven to 400°F. Line a baking sheet with parchment paper or a silicone baking mat.

2) In a medium bowl, beat the egg whites, coconut aminos or tamari, salt, and white pepper. Add the chicken and let marinate for 10 to 15 minutes.

3) MAKE THE CRUST: Meanwhile, in a food processor, combine the flour, flaxseed, pumpkin seeds, sunflower seeds, salt, paprika, and onion powder. Pulse until the mixture forms a bread crumb–like consistency. Transfer the mixture to a gallon-size resealable plastic bag.

4) Remove the chicken from the egg mixture and transfer them to the bag with the crust mixture. Seal the bag and shake to coat chicken thoroughly.

5) Place the coated chicken tenders on the prepared baking sheet and mist with cooking spray. Bake for 15 to 20 minutes, until golden brown.

6) MAKE THE DIPPING SAUCE: Meanwhile, in a small bowl, whisk together all the dipping sauce ingredients.

7) Serve the chicken tenders with the dipping sauce and maybe low-sugar ketchup on the side.

GREEK-STYLE BAKED COD

Imagine yourself on the island of Santorini, sipping a cold glass of something delicious and taking in the whitewashed houses punctuated by piercing blue roofs. The warm sun caresses your face and you gasp at the unctuous waft of yumminess with a hint of licorice that floats across your nose when this Greek-Style Baked Cod shows up at your table. Oh, wait, you cooked it.

INGREDIENTS

2 garlic cloves, crushed

1 tablespoon extra-virgin olive oil

1 tablespoon fresh oregano leaves, or 1½ teaspoons dried

1½ tablespoons fresh lemon juice

¼ cup ouzo (optional, but trust me, it is amazing)

1 teaspoon Himalayan pink salt

1 teaspoon freshly ground black pepper

1½ lbs wild-caught codfish fillets

Nonstick olive or coconut oil cooking spray

½ cup finely chopped red onion

10 kalamata olives, pitted and finely chopped

DIRECTIONS

1) In a large bowl, combine the garlic, olive oil, oregano, lemon juice, ouzo, salt, and pepper. Add the fish, cover, and marinate for at least 1 hour.

2) Preheat the oven to 350°F. Spray a baking dish with cooking spray.

3) Transfer the fish to the prepared baking dish and top with the onion and olives. Bake for 25 to 30 minutes, until the fish is cooked through and nicely opaque in color. Serve with roasted veggies and Heirloom Tomato Salad (page 36) for an armchair trip to the Mediterranean.

GINGER AND CARROT MEATBALLS

It doesn't matter what planet you came from, ain't a soul I've ever met who's above a genuinely amazing meatball. And the hint of ground ginger with the carrot in these is a winner, winner meatball dinner. These will become a go-to, on rotation.

INGREDIENTS

1 pound ground free-range beef, chicken, or turkey

¼ cup Mexican-style chorizo

¼ cup ground golden flaxmeal

2 egg whites

1 teaspoon ground ginger

¼ cup finely grated carrot

2 large garlic cloves, minced

2 tablespoons minced fresh cilantro leaves

1 tablespoon olive oil

½ teaspoon kosher salt

Freshly ground black pepper

Nonstick olive or coconut oil cooking spray

½ cup prepared low-sodium bone broth

DIRECTIONS

1) Line a rimmed baking sheet with a silicone baking pad.

2) In a large bowl, combine the ground beef, chorizo, flaxmeal, egg whites, ginger, carrot, garlic, cilantro, olive oil, and salt, season with pepper, and mix with clean hands until well incorporated.

3) Using a small ice cream scoop or your hands, roll the meat mixture into roughly 1½-inch balls. Place them on the prepared baking sheet and mist them with cooking spray.

4) Heat a large skillet over medium-high heat. Add the meatballs and cook, rolling them in the pan so all surfaces are cooked, until browned, about 5 minutes. Add the broth to the bottom of the pan, reduce the heat to medium, cover, and cook for 8 to 10 minutes, until the meatballs are completely cooked through. If you like them a little more browned, you can finish them under the broiler for 2 minutes.

5) Serve alongside a mushroom farro risotto or on a bed of zucchini noodles and a grating of Parmesan cheese for a real "sketti and meatballs kinda" meal.

BLUEBERRY VANILLA CHIA SEED PUDDING

What could be better than eating pudding for breakfast and having it basically make itself? Plus, blueberries and chia seeds together are an antioxidant power couple. Just get yourself set up with some mason jars you can grab and go. That's good news to spoon to!

INGREDIENTS

2 cups unsweetened almond milk or other nondairy milk

½ teaspoon pure vanilla extract

1 cup fresh or frozen blueberries

2 teaspoons granulated stevia or monkfruit extract

6 tablespoons chia seeds

1½ tablespoons unsweetened shredded coconut

DIRECTIONS

1) In a blender, combine the almond milk, vanilla, blueberries, and stevia.

2) Put 1½ tablespoons of the chia seeds into each of four mason jars. Evenly distribute the blueberry-milk mixture over the top of each and stir or shake well. Seal the jars and refrigerate for at least 6 hours or ideally overnight, until thickened.

3) Top each with about 1 teaspoon of the coconut and enjoy cold.

STRAWBERRY COCONUT NICE CREAM

I scream, you scream, we all scream for nice cream! When you go "nice," you never go back. It doesn't matter if you're not a full-time vegan—this will become your go-to dessert for every day of the week. With just five ingredients, it couldn't be any easier. Scoop it, spoon it, and love it up.

INGREDIENTS

2 (14-ounce) cans unsweetened full-fat coconut milk

4 cups sliced fresh or frozen strawberries

1 vanilla bean, split lengthwise and seeds scraped out (see Note)

2 frozen bananas, peel left on (see page 99)

1 teaspoon granulated stevia

OPTIONAL TOPPINGS

Unsweetened shredded coconut

Cacao nibs

Crushed walnuts

DIRECTIONS

1) Refrigerate the cans of coconut milk overnight. Open each can and scoop only the thick, white coconut cream into a large bowl or the bowl of a stand mixer fitted with the whisk attachment; discard the watery liquid left in the can or refrigerate it for another use (it's good for smoothies!). Whip the coconut cream using a handheld mixer or the stand mixer until it holds soft peaks.

2) In a food processor, combine 3 cups of the strawberries, vanilla, banana, stevia, and sea salt. Pulse until smooth.

3) Fold the strawberry mixture into the coconut whipped cream. Gently add the remaining sliced strawberries. Transfer the mixture to a lidded freezer-safe storage container and use the back of a spoon to level the top. Cover and freeze for 2 hours.

4) Scoop the mixture out with a spoon to "un-ice." (You can also transfer it to the food processor and pulse until smooth.) Return the mixture to the container, cover, and freeze until solid. The goal is to get the creamiest consistency possible.

5) When you're ready to eat, take the nice cream out and let it soften at room temperature for 5 to 10 minutes before scooping. Spoon into bowls, top as desired, and serve.

NOTE: The whole vanilla bean makes it extra special, but you can use 1 teaspoon pure vanilla extract instead.

THE 90/10
RULE

Have Your Pasta and Eat It, Too

Let's fantasize for a second. I want you to think about your all-time favorite meal. Like, if you had one meal left on planet Earth, what would it be? Let me guess. It's a meal you would consider "unhealthy," right? Okay, hold on to that thought for a second. Since we're playing sharesies, I'll disclose mine.

I dreamily recall a fund-raiser event I attended for the American Cancer Society in Los Angeles, where several prominent chefs were offering their best bites. My silent-auction item of a catered dinner for six had just been sold to the highest bidder—actress Allison Janney. Feeling like I was already on an all-time high after bantering with my new much taller BFF, I eagerly scoped out the offerings. I guiltily accepted a small plate of delicate triangles of pillowy pasta filled with succulent morsels of buttery lobster tail, topped with shavings of Parmigiano-Reggiano and an opulent crown of sublime black truffles. *Pasta?!* I thought. *Who eats pasta anymore? It's carbs after all, and isn't consuming them in LA a sin?* I took a deep inhale, and gasped. I'm fairly certain the earth stopped rotating. The birds hushed; the crickets stopped chirping. The air stood still, and my peripheral vision disappeared. As the first bite fell on my tongue, my heart felt warm—and I think I may have let out a groan. It was love, true love, and I didn't care who knew it.

That plate of two beautifully folded pieces of pasta, made with semolina flour and water, so perfectly executed, became my new muse. I ate them ever so slowly, tasting each bite with every ounce of my being. Even though there were twenty other incredible food offerings with no limit on how many servings I could take, I was satiated. That's all I ate. I wanted nothing else. It was so damn good, my pleasure meter went through the roof in seconds, and I couldn't even think of following it up with anything else. That's when it hit me like a giant pizza: *Could it be that our perspective is what's out of whack?*

Without hesitation, I ate the *forkin'* pasta, and I do it again, and again, and again, every single week.

And so can you.

That special "last meal" you so affectionately recalled? You can still have that, with a level of frequency that will surprise you. The key is to understand and implement the other seven core food strategies first so you reshape how you process, taste, and enjoy what you're feeding your body.

La Dolcissima Vita—The Forking Good Life

I had the good fortune of studying abroad in Italy and have spent a lot of time there since my introduction to the greatest place on earth for studying foodies. Italians love to eat, and carbs, dairy, and meat are mainstays, yet you'd be hard-pressed to find anyone on a diet. Here's some of the key intel I gleaned over the years:

- **The dairy for fresh mozzarella, Parmigiano-Reggiano, and other cheeses comes from animals that are fed the right nourishment and raised without added hormones. The result is a superior flavor, so much so that pizza is never covered in mounds of cheese, just enough to spread some love.**
- **Flour is milled locally and breads are baked with painstaking care using fermented starters versus quick-rise yeasts. This yields a much more gut-friendly product that's easier to digest, without bleached or other-wise processed ingredients, stabilizers, or fillers.**

- The portions are much, much smaller. Italians will eat three courses, but we're not talking about bottomless plates of pasta. A meal starts with two or three ounces of cooked pasta, about the same portion of protein, and ends with vegetables. You leave the table feeling satisfied, not like a stuffed turkey.
- I've never seen a 64-ounce tumbler of soda in anyone's hand—ever.
- People take their time eating. Gulping down your food whole like Homer Simpson is a sure way to bad gut health. Don't discount the importance of digestion and breaking down food properly. With carbs, it starts in your mouth with your saliva, which is why your mama always told you to chew slowly.
- You tend to eat far less when you're in the company of others than when you eat alone. Italians love to eat in groups, with gusto, wholly engaged in the act.
- I didn't see a whole lot of snacking happening or people pulling up to fast food windows and scarfing down food in their Alfa Romeos.
- While *venti* is, in fact, the Italian word for "twenty," 20-ounce coffee drinks with over 100 grams of sugar do not exist there.

That, my friends, is living the sweetest life—*la dolcissima vita*—but without the sugar. It's on the tip of your tongue, and you can train it to take care of you and your health. Ingredients shouldn't come with a laundry list of unpronounceable ingredients manufactured in a lab. It should be enjoyed with fervor and savored like something that leaves us waiting for the next meal with giddy anticipation like your first time at Disneyland. It should be enjoyed in serving sizes proportionate to your caloric expenditures. It should be nutritionally balanced. It can and should include carbs. #bestnewsevah!

So where do your decadent indulgences play into this melody of carnal joy? It's called the 90/10 rule, and it means, quite simply, balance: 90 percent of your meals will adhere to the other seven core strategies and the remaining 10 percent can be whatever you like. The oldest story in the world relating to food begins with an apple tree, a naked man and woman, and a command: "Don't eat from that tree." What did they do? They ate from the ding-dang tree.

With this strategy, you can eat from the tree every week without falling into food damnation.

Did I just see you twerk with abandon?

Here's how forgiving your body and metabolism are, and what bodybuilders and figure competitors have known and practiced for ages. Your FBIQ actually does better when you indulge a little throughout the week. To break down the science, the other seven strategies you have been practicing in this book were designed to help you regulate your hormones and keep your blood sugar on track to avoid spikes and falls. Leptin is a hormone that helps regulate appetite and recognizes fullness. Now that you've shifted into a place where you've taught your body to be efficient and burn fat and calories like a well-oiled machine, you're ready to embrace the 90/10 rule, because now your 10% meals will actually increase leptin levels for a short period of time. Your body will then go into overtime to burn up those extra calories and fat. This works especially well when you are eating carbs.

Some people refer to the 10% as "cheat meals," but I'm not a fan of that term. Cheating equates to guilt. You're not cheating yourself. It's a purposeful way of supercharging your own fantastic machine's FBIQ. Can I get a "woot woot" for a guilt-free 10%?! When you intermittently boost your caloric intake, your body burns more calories instead of plateauing and adjusting. You actually need this 10% wiggle room to boost your FBIQ, but you also need it for your pleasure center—the one that allows you to indulge a little.

So let's define a little. . . . If you are eating about five times per day, thirty-five times per week, 10% means about three meals per week can be what you want them to be. Maybe a serving of your favorite pancakes, pasta, a piece of birthday cake, a slice of pizza. It's not a four-person serving of ravioli, not the whole cake, and not the whole pizza. Allow yourself to take a few meals a week, without guilt or saying to yourself, "I'm so bad." The science shows that if you up your calories in consecutive days, it's even more effective, so how about we keep the 10% for the weekends and have something even more exciting to look forward to on Monday? #MondayMotivation

The Rules of 90/10 Engagement

Just like the other seven strategies you've eaten through, the 90/10 rule requires some prethought and planning, or else you'll end up in the oh-no-I'm-out-of-control zone. I want you to think of this as your opportunity to really enjoy something you love, because it's special and it gives you joy. When I ate that lobster-filled handmade semolina pasta ravioli with shaved truffles, something viscerally changed in me. My heart exploded. I heard angels sing and felt things I've never felt before. I only needed a few bites because they were enough. Even if you wanted to eat the whole sheet of double fudge brownies, you probably couldn't gorge on those foods like you used to. You will find that because you've retrained yourself (and your taste buds) in your approach to food, it won't take much to get you to that pleasure point. Don't count the bites. Make every bite count.

Don't count the bites—make every bite count.

EIGHT WAYS TO KEEP YOUR 90/10 LIFE IN CHECK

1. Plan your 10% meals like your 90% meals.
2. Plan your 10%er for Friday, Saturday, and Sunday.
3. Remember, it's a meal, not a day of wild food orgies.
4. Calories should be about 15 percent (around 200–300 for the average woman, 250–350 for the average man) extra on days you have a 10% meal.
5. Make it good; savor it slowly.
6. Hydrate well.
7. Don't bring junk home you wouldn't want to wake up with.
8. Share the goodies with someone you like or love.

I remember hearing Oprah say, "When you have something that you know is going to taste soooo good, it's so much better to share it so both of you will say, 'That was soooo good.'" I always say #sharingiscaring—and it helps you control how much you eat. If the average restaurant meal is 1,000 calories, that's half the calories the average woman needs in an entire day!

When YOU aren't controlling your portion sizes, restaurants are. You should always consider the size of the meal being put in front of you. If you eat out, remember: You don't have to eat the whole thing. Keep those 10%ers to something you really want to enjoy, and eat them slowly, savoring every forking-good bite.

When making more decadent desserts at home, I like to use automatic portion control by baking individual cupcakes, crisps, and pies in a muffin pan, ramekins, or cupcake liners. I love using them for dishes like mac 'n' cheese, au gratin potatoes mixed with kohlrabi, or stuffing made with farro.

The key here is to enjoy every bite you take. Eat some, share some. Studies show that when you eat with others, you tend to eat less. So enjoy with the people you love.

FORKING-GOOD POLENTA LASAGNA

My daughter insisted that this recipe be included. In fact, she asked me three times. I think she likes it a lot. Don't even turn your nose up at the idea of using polenta from a tube, either. It replaces doughy noodles in this *forkin' good* rendition and fam fave, and you'll thank me when you taste it. Use organic polenta, because corn is one of those highly GMO crops—along with wheat and soy—so it's important to seek out the organic kind.

INGREDIENTS

Nonstick olive or coconut oil cooking spray

1 teaspoon extra-virgin olive oil

1 eggplant, unpeeled, cut into small dice

2 medium zucchini, cut into small dice

½ teaspoon kosher salt

½ teaspoon freshly ground black pepper

12 ounces spinach

1½ cups prepared organic Italian-style tomato sauce

½ cup fresh basil

1 (14-ounce) tube prepared organic polenta, cut into ¼-inch-thick slices

1½ cups shredded mozzarella cheese

DIRECTIONS

1) Preheat the oven to 450°F. Coat a 9 x 13-inch baking dish with cooking spray.

2) In a large nonstick skillet, heat the olive oil over medium-high heat. Add the eggplant, zucchini, salt, and pepper and cook, stirring occasionally, until the vegetables are tender and just beginning to brown, 4 to 6 minutes. Add ½ cup water and the spinach; cover and cook until wilted, stirring once, about 3 minutes.

3) Stir in the tomato sauce and heat through, 1 to 2 minutes. Remove from the heat and stir in the basil.

4) Place the polenta slices in a single layer in the prepared baking dish, trimming them to fit if necessary. Top with the eggplant and zuchinni mixture and sprinkle with the cheese. Bake until bubbling and the cheese has just melted, about 15 minutes. Let stand for 5 to 10 minutes before serving.

BISON KOFTA BURGERS

INGREDIENTS

3 garlic cloves, minced

3 tablespoons finely minced red onion

2 tablespoons finely minced fresh cilantro

2 tablespoons coconut amino acids or tamari

1 pound ground bison or grass-fed beef

1 tablespoon ground coriander

2 teaspoons ground cumin

1 teaspoon smoked sea salt

½ teaspoon cayenne pepper

½ teaspoon freshly ground black pepper

OPTIONAL TOPPINGS

Grilled onions

Sliced tomato

Quickles (page 76)

Lettuce

Sliced avocado

Feta cheese

Yogurt sauce

DIRECTIONS

1) Heat a grill to medium.

2) In a large bowl, stir together the garlic, onion, cilantro, and coconut aminos. Add the ground bison and mix with clean hands to combine. Add the coriander, cumin, salt, cayenne, and black pepper and mix until evenly distributed.

3) Form the meat mixture into 3½- to 4-inch patties, about ½ inch thick. Grill for 6 to 7 minutes on each side for a medium-well burger, or to your desired doneness.

4) Serve with the toppings of your choice. I like to serve the toppings set up in a little salad bar so everyone can customize their own burger.

OVEN-FRIED CHICKEN

You won't miss the fat from these breasts, wings, legs, and thighs—or the chicken's, either!

INGREDIENTS

2 cups buttermilk

1 tablespoon Dijon mustard

1 whole 3- to 4-lb free-range organic chicken, cut into serving pieces

1½ cups ground flaxseed

1 teaspoon cayenne pepper

1 teaspoon ground oregano

1 tablespoon onion powder

1 tablespoon garlic powder

2 tablespoons freshly ground black pepper

1 teaspoon sea salt

Nonstick olive or coconut oil cooking spray

DIRECTIONS

1) In a medium bowl, whisk together the buttermilk and the mustard. Immerse the chicken pieces in the buttermilk mixture and soak for at least 30 minutes and up to 2 hours.

2) Preheat the oven to 400°F. Line a baking sheet with a silicone baking pad.

3) Combine the flaxseed, cayenne, oregano, onion powder, garlic powder, black pepper, and salt on a flat plate. Remove chicken pieces from the buttermilk and shake off all excess liquid. Roll the chicken pieces in the flax-spice mixture until well coated.

4) Place the chicken on the prepared baking sheet and mist with cooking spray. Cover the baking sheet with aluminum foil to keep moisture in.

5) Bake for about 40 minutes, removing the foil for the final 10 to 15 minutes, until the chicken is golden brown and a thermometer inserted into the thickest part (without touching bone) registers at least 165°F.

MACADAMIA NUT BANANA PANCAKES WITH COCONUT SYRUP

For me, this is Hawaii on a plate. There is nothing more decadently delicious than the combination of buttery, rich macadamia nuts with bananas and coconut syrup. Just thinking about this right now makes me want to cry, it's so delicious. Takes Jack Johnson's "Banana Pancakes" song to the next level.

MACADAMIA NUT BANANA PANCAKES

1½ cups all-purpose gluten-free flour

¼ teaspoon kosher salt

½ teaspoon baking soda

¾ teaspoon baking powder

3 large eggs

2 cups unsweetened almond milk or coconut milk

2 medium-large very ripe bananas, peels on (see Note, page 99)

1 teaspoon pure vanilla extract

½ cup chopped macadamia nuts

COCONUT SYRUP

1 (14-ounce) can unsweetened full-fat coconut milk

1 tablespoon arrowroot powder or cornstarch

½ cup simple syrup (see Note)

DIRECTIONS

1) MAKE THE PANCAKES: In a large bowl, stir together the flour, salt, baking soda, and baking powder.

2) Place the eggs, almond milk, bananas, and vanilla in a blender. Blend on the lowest speed just until the mixture is smooth.

3) Add the wet ingredients to the flour mixture and whisk together until smooth. Stir in the macadamia nuts.

4) On a hot griddle, drop the batter in ¼ cups. Once the tops begin to bubble, flip the pancakes and cook on other side until golden. Transfer to a plate and repeat with the remaining batter.

5) MAKE THE COCONUT SYRUP: In a medium saucepan, whisk together the coconut milk and arrowroot powder until smooth. Add the simple syrup and bring to a boil; reduce the heat to low and simmer for 10 minutes. Let cool for 5 to 10 minutes before pouring over pancakes. It will thicken up further as it cools.

NOTE: For the simple syrup, stir together equal parts sweetener and water (e.g., ½ cup monk fruit extract dissolved in ½ cup water).

DARK CHOCOLATE AVOCADO MOUSSE WITH RASPBERRY COULIS AND COCONUT WHIP

RASPBERRY COULIS

1 cup fresh raspberries

1 teaspoon granulated stevia

2 teaspoons fresh lemon juice

DARK CHOCOLATE AVOCADO MOUSSE

1 large ripe avocado

¼ cup unsweetened cocoa powder

¼ cup unsweetened almond milk or coconut milk (or rice milk, for a nut-free option)

¼ cup granulated stevia

OPTIONAL TOPPINGS

Coconut whip topping, raspberries, blueberries, all-natural coconut whipped cream, star fruit slices, slivered almonds, unsweetened shredded coconut, dusting of ground cinnamon and/ or unsweetened cocoa powder—or any combination of these that your heart desires!

DIRECTIONS

1) MAKE THE COULIS: In a small saucepan, combine the raspberries, stevia, and ½ cup water and bring to a boil. Reduce the heat to low and cook for about 10 minutes. Remove from the heat and push the mixture through a fine-mesh strainer into a clean bowl. Whisk in the lemon juice. Let cool to room temperature.

2) MAKE THE MOUSSE: Halve and pit the avocado. Scoop the avocado flesh out of the skin using a spoon and drop it into a food processor. Pulse the avocado until smooth.

3) Add the cocoa powder, almond milk, stevia, and ½ cup water and pulse again until completely blended and smooth.

4) Evenly distribute the mousse among four martini glasses, champagne flutes, ramekins, or mason jars and divide the raspberry coulis among them. Chill for at least 1 hour before serving.

5) Before serving, top as desired and eat it up with a spoon!

CONVERTIBLE MEALS

Wouldn't you like to just drop the top and roll when it comes time to eat? Travel around the world with a single bite? Now that you've gotten a handle on the eight essential strategies that build a vibrant, healthy, superstar food foundation for your most awesome life, it's time to put it all together. With this strategy, all you need are core ingredients that you can assemble into beautiful, nourishing meals within minutes, meals that feed your vibrancy, your mind, your soul, and your healthy appetite. This isn't about deprivation or what I call sad food—no color, no texture, no flavor, and no fun. Food should feel, taste, and look appetizing, and these options won't let you down.

The Convertible Meals strategy includes prewashed and prepped core ingredients, including veggies, single-ingredient grains, proteins, and fats, along with dressings, key pantry staples, and nutrient-dense add-ons to create this mix-and-match approach. The ease of convertible meals depends on a weekly Meal-Prep Power Hour. This includes prewashing and chopping up your produce, cooking super grains and proteins, preparing fat fillers, and stocking up on dense add-ons. If you can dedicate one hour a week to prep, you can get through a lot of your meal setup. This way, you've got "prêt-à-manger" ingredients ready to go. All the meal prep is done and the ingredients available. You choose the meal form you most want at that time.

By enjoying five meals a day, each typically made up of 300 to 500 calories, you'll never, ever be hungry or, worse, hangry.

THE CONVERTIBLE MEALS APPROACH

1. Helps you maintain healthy blood sugar levels.
2. Keeps you from feeling "stuffed" and unmotivated.
3. Aids your digestion with smaller portions, so it's not overloaded.
4. Helps you portion out your nutrients so you avoid energy slumps.
5. Lets you change things up and avoid boredom with mix-and-match ingredients.

The Meal-Prep Power Hour is a once-a-week system for getting ingredients prepped so you can put together your core meal forms. This is multitasking at its finest, my friends, because there's a strategy to the method. In about an hour, you can get your fridge humming and make mealtime super simple:

Here's the meal-prep road map:

VEGGIES

- Pick 4 to 8 nonstarchy veggies for the week. Half of those should be leafy greens.
- Pick 2 or 3 starchy veggies for the week.
- Bake sweet potatoes and other root veggies that take a lot of time in the oven.
- Chop produce in the food processor with the right attachment and store in containers.

PROTEINS

- Pick 2 or 3 for the week.
- Pick a spice blend, marinade, or dressing and layer your proteins with big flavor.
- Cook them in a slow cooker, in the oven, or on the grill.

SUPER GRAINS

- Pick 1 or 2 for the week.
- Cook them in a pot on the stovetop or in a rice cooker, using one of the cooking-liquid ideas mentioned in Strategy 5.

FAT FILLERS

- Pick 2 or 3 for the week.
- Prioritize plant-based fats, including nuts, seeds, and avocados; add omega-3 rich seafood.

DENSE ADD-ONS

- Pick 2 or 3 for the week.
- Store these in easy-to-access containers so they're in sight.

You can take your prepped ingredients and transform them into four different vehicles. These include:

REV YOUR ENGINE: Hot and Cold Bowls
STREET SMART: Wraps
FUEL EFFICIENT: Salads
HIGH OCTANE: Stuffed Meals

You use the same core ingredients to create different meals, just by mixing up the seasonings, combinations, and toppings. You'll never get bored when life takes over and you have to shift into overdrive.

Don't we all wish we could sit down and enjoy a civilized meal with white napkins, classical music playing, and lively conversation for hours? Then real life happens, and you have somewhere to be 10 minutes ago. Time to roll! You can do this without the stressful need to feed with a little prep work.

- Have some cup-size containers filled with snacking veggies, mixed berries, apple slices, and protein balls on hand for easily grabbing to take with you on the go. You could line these up in your fridge and get in the habit of making sure these turbo-boosters are ready to go on the fly.
- Instead of bread and flour tortillas, make sandwich fillings "street smart" and portable by rolling them up in: Cabbage leaves; romaine, butter, and/or iceberg lettuce leaves; nori sheets; kohlrabi (it's a veggie), or jicama, cut into tortilla-thin discs.
- Hard-boil a bunch of eggs, and when you're ready to eat, sauté them in a little ghee and ground cumin, salt, and pepper to heat them (they'll explode in the microwave).
- Pre-portion snack bags with fat-filler blends and stash them in your pantry, car, purse, and computer bag.

0 to 60 with No Emissions

One of the best things you can do to save money and time is to use every bit of your fresh food, from seed to stalk. By bringing your produce home and cleaning it before you store it, you'll help it last longer and you'll also get a good assessment of what you've got to fuel up with for the week. When your precious veggies are stored in plastic bags and stuffed into the crisper, they quite literally suffocate and die prematurely. Getting them prepped to eat will help you get meals on the table like a racing pit crew, and get you hauling ass on your way to doing all those awesome things you have on your proverbial plate.

Aside from composting, there are probably some things you're used to doing or throwing out when you're getting your food ready that you might want to reconsider:

- **CITRUS PEELS: If you don't zest your citrus, you're losing out on a ton of concentrated flavor. Grapefruit, orange, mandarin, lemon, lime, and all the other yummy citrus fruit oils offer a nice little mood lift! Use a Microplane or citrus zester to get the goods off easily. Once you're done, peels can get dehydrated and steeped into hot or iced tea. If you're not going to use them in your cooking, put them into your garbage disposal for a little burst of fresh citrus smell.**

- **VEGGIE SKINS:** In most cases, the skin is where there's a ton of fiber and nutrients. Root veggies can keep theirs on, as long as they're given a good cleanin'.
- **BANANA PEELS:** If you're making a smoothie, leave the peel ON your banana and throw it into the blender. It'll give the smoothie a nice frothiness and adds a lot of nutrition, too. The riper the banana, the sweeter the peel, so don't give up on it if it's gone past its prime. And just think of all those peels you're keeping out of the landfills—billions of pounds are thrown away every year. Now you're wearing your smarty pants.
- **PARMESAN CHEESE RIND:** Instead of tossing the rinds, add them to broths and soups as they're cooking. They add a deep, rich flavor and a nice, subtle cheesiness without going overboard. I first learned about this from my fabulous Italian friend's personal chef when I was in college and we were staying in her sixteenth-century Tuscan castle for the summer. Never had it so good, lemme tell ya.
- **VEGGIE TRIMMINGS:** Stalks, leaves, and even roots can go into soups and broths for added flavor and nutrient density. The roots are where the plant's life is connected to its life force! Eat it up.

If it looks like your fruit, veggies, and herbs are getting past their prime, it's a good idea to puree and freeze them. Avocado, berries, sweet potatoes, leafy greens, and herbs are all great candidates for this. You can store them in sandwich or snack bags to make it easy to throw the purees into baked goods, soups, stews, and sautés. Isn't it the worst when a recipe calls for fresh herbs and you use 1/32 of the bunch? You can use an ice cube tray to portion them out and add some ghee, coconut oil, or olive oil; freeze them and pop in a cube of flavor when you're cooking up eggs, veggies, or proteins.

By now you know that my focus is on ingredients, flavors, and textures, but one surefire way to remake any meal is to convert it. Spice blends, sauces, and dressings accessorize the dish and pull it all together when it comes to varying the feel and flavor of the meal. One night, it could be a tamari, lime, and lemongrass dipping sauce to transform a rice paper wrap, or a spice blend with cumin, coriander, and sumac for a salad bowl. In an instant, you've become a world traveler without ever reinventing the main ingredients. Toss proteins with a spice blend or switch up the "be real dense" add-ons for a whole new dish every time.

In the chart on the next page, you'll get some sample Meal-Prep Power Hour combos that'll get you going quicker than a fast food drive-through.

CONVERTIBLE MEAL EXAMPLE

CORE INGREDIENTS: PREP THESE ONCE AND ENJOY IN A VARIETY OF WAYS ALL WEEK LONG

VEGETABLES:	GRAIN:	FAT:	PROTEIN:	FLAVOR BOOSTERS:
1 cup greens (baby spinach or kale) and ½ cup mixed raw shredded carrots and beets	¼ cup cooked quinoa or kaniweh; millet, black rice, or farro (cooked in low-sodium stock for added flavor)	2 tablespoons hemp seeds, sunflower seeds, chia seeds, nuts, or avocado	up to 4 oz. grilled salmon or chicken, sautéed ground turkey, or broiled tempeh; unsweetened milk	1 teaspoon Spice blend or 2 tablespoons dressing
WRAPS:	SALAD BOWL:	HOT BOWL:	ENTRÉE:	BREAKFAST BOWL OR SMOOTHIE:
Butter lettuce or romaine wraps filled with vegetables; grain, fat, and protein above plus choice of dressing or spice blend	Vegetables above plus additional cup of your choice of greens and any additional non-starchy veggies; grain, fat, and protein plus choice of dressing or spice blend	Vegetables, fat, protein, and 2 servings of grains, heated, plus choice of dressing or spice blend	Bell pepper stuffed with greens, grain, choice of fat and protein above, cooked in oven plus choice of dressing or spice blend	Breakfast Bowl: 2 servings of grains, fat, and unsweetened almond, coconut, or your favorite nondairy milk plus 2 chopped dates Smoothie: Greens, fats, unsweetened almond, coconut or your favorite nondairy milk plus 2 chopped dates

SPICE BLENDS, DRESSINGS, AND MARINADES

STORE IN SPICE CONTAINERS FOR CONVENIENCE

MedMex Spice Blend (makes 4 servings)	Toss together: 2 tablespoons ground cumin, 2 tablespoons ground coriander, 1 tablespoon granulated garlic, 1 teaspoon sumac
Provençale Spice Blend (makes 4 servings)	Toss together: 2 tablespoons dried tarragon, 1 tablespoon dried lavender, 1 teaspoon Himalayan pink salt, ½ teaspoon dried lemon zest
Zenned Out Dressing (makes 2 servings)	Whisk together: 3 tablespoons avocado oil, 1 tablespoon toasted sesame oil, 1 teaspoon ground ginger, 1 raw apple cider vinegar, 2 teaspoons amino acids, ½ teaspoon organic granulated stevia
Real Ranch Dressing	See recipe
Romesco Sauce	See recipe
Roasted Red Pepper Pesto	See Recipe
Real Dish Dressing (page 26)	See recipe

EAT LIKE
YOU GIVE A FORK

We need very few things to survive. Thank the Lord food is one of them. Now that you've been through the eight strategies of *Eat Like You Give a Fork*, you know why this is not only a survival skill, but also a thriving skill. We are omnivores with opposable thumbs. We are the only creatures capable of alchemy in the kitchen. That makes us all kitchen magicians. It's not about pulling a rabbit out of a hat. It's much more realistic and attainable when you have a plan and your taste buds in shape.

Cooking connects us to our humanity. Whether as simple as a salad or as intricate as a four-course meal, the fact that we can articulate food into art, appreciate it with all five senses, and enjoy it with others is nothing short of a miracle.

We have the conscious choice to select what we will eat, then prepare it, consume it, and share it. We can pick certain foods that contain superior health and flavor properties and combine them in a way that nourishes our cells. We use chemistry to nurture a creation into being by using heat, cold, spice, a blender, or a knife.

We can invite friends and family to the table and fill it with laughter and conviviality. Or we can choose to eat alone, and depending on how much time we have, we can spend a few minutes or a few hours indulging in the meal. If the mood takes us, we can set out some nice dishes and silverware; fancy up the table with pretty place mats, candles, and some flowers; put on background music; and serve some wine and maybe even an assortment of drinks. We're able to make a meal look appealing, not to Instagram it, but because it makes us feel joy. No other creature does this. On the flip side mealtime can rely on processed convenience foods full of empty calories, empty promises, and words we can't pronounce. It can be a chore or a haven, an inconvenience or something we anticipate with great excitement. It can be a beautiful, sumptuous gift from the earth, full of real color, real value, and real intention. How we source it, prepare it, savor it, share it, and make memories with it is ours for the taking.

At that point, we've created another layer of alchemy. In Arabic, we call it *mezhag*, or "zest for life," infusing our creative touch to make them special—because when we look back on our lives, it's not the calories that count. It's the moments.

Have I rocked your world? Well, at least I hope I've rotated your plate.

From this point on, we will uphold a *Forkin'* food constitution, and for this, we have a preamble:

To these dishes we hold so dear
United we eat
Together we protein ball
And if a moment comes upon us
Where we lose our way
And find our taste buds led astray
Into a bag of chips, cookies, or a hot fudge sundae binge
We will not resign or become unhinged
Instead, rise again, another morning to slay
Our eight strategies in hand, good habits here to stay
We'll eat our way to vitality
Starting with breakfast and VitaliTea
Nothing will stop us from pursuing good health; it's our duty
You'll Eat Like You Give a Fork now, and let me say, nice booty.

Even if yesterday wasn't perfect, what you choose today marks the the start of the real you. With your eight essential food strategies, a reconditioned palate, and a new wardrobe of recipes and sustainable habits on lock, just eat, rinse, repeat—and keep feeding that vital, energized, youthful, forking amazing bod of yours. Just keep your eyes on your BAG, and you can eat your way through anything. Remember:

Eat tons o' fresh low-starch veggies.
Eat raw.
Eat regularly.
Eat slowly.
Eat balanced macronutrients.
Eat high-quality foods.
Eat with intention and gratitude.
Eat with the people you love.

You hot dish, you!

INDEX